HOW TO PLAY
WINNING
DARTS

HOW TO PLAY WINNING DARTS

By

Ralph Maus

A DART PLAYER'S BIBLE
Buddy
STRAD DARTS

Printed in the United States of America
Second Edition
10 9 8 7 6 5 4 3 2

Library of Congress cataloging-in-Publication Data

Maus, (Buddy) Ralph.
How to Play Winning Darts/Buddy.
Including combined index and table of contents/sketches
1. Darts (Game). 2. How to methods. Title
794.3   # 92-85007

5 Washington St., Westborough, MA 01581-1012

ABOUT THE BOOK

Many believe Darts (today) is the world's fastest growing indoor sport. Yet, until now, players saw few 'how to'facts. Books focused mainly on dart history, the game's stars, world records, other games, rules, etc. Dart players looking to improve their game, saw few clues.

"WINNING DARTS" takes an important step in filling the void for fans of a unique, exciting sport. The book will: Introduce you to winning Darts, help you play to the best of your abilities. It shows ways to hone needed skills with sound hands-on drills to spot and fix faults.

Most important, knowing the ropes, you can feel and act like a WINNER, no matter who throws the final dart. Love for the game and knowing you gave your best yields this outlook.

<u>DEDICATION</u>

TO WILLIAM & IRMA M. (BAKER) MAUS AND RICHARD ALLAN MAUS. THANKS ALSO TO MY TUTORS PAUL LIM, LARRY BUTLER AND ALL THE OTHERS UNABLE TO THROW JUST ONE.

AUTHORS' COMMENTS:

I held some doubts about writing a book. Still, the venture proved a labor of love—each word a joy. I felt it vital every darter (old and new) should find a source of game proven facts! The idea of helping other darters thrills me. I feel right concerning the thirteen plus years spent on a much-needed manual. Clearly, *MY* own outlook and game improved.

My writing will never dazzle anyone. Yet, I can show you how to play winning Darts. You may ask, "if I can give great advice, why am I not a pro?" Two reasons.

First, Knowing 'how to do it' does not mean one owns the ability, or ever will. No matter, you can still enjoy the game. Weaker players, by thinking, do beat excellent shooters. Too sure of their finesse, stronger rivals often make mistakes.

Second, Two points, really. AGE: Darts did not find me until I neared 50. Then, as I peaked, an ACCIDENT disabled me. I can still win in 'A' league play, but now consider playing Darts a feat.

You may not agree with all my views and methods. I respect your opinions, remaining open to any comments. Please write! No person can possibly know every fine point of Darts. The task may never truly be complete. Yet, "*WINNING DARTS*" hits all the necessary points. Armed with enough new facts, I would issue an updated version.

AUTHOR'S NOTES:

GENDER: Read she and he to mean any person! I mean *NO* bias. Both men and women are very important to Darts.

MOTION & MOVEMENT: Two hazy words I became lost trying to separate were motion and movement. Wordbooks are vague about their usage. Reading the meanings, one cannot tell the two words apart. Ignoring rules, I gave each word a clear Darts meaning.

MOTION, is using *only* the arm and hand to throw a dart at a target **ON** demand—*positive* actions.

MOVEMENT, is any flaw causing the body to **MOVE** as you throw, swaying prevents hitting the target. The main cause of this *negative* action is poor habits and faulty methods.

BRAIN & MIND: Two more words given exact meanings.

THE BRAIN has wisdom beyond your reach. The brain controls the body. You cannot (usually) tap the brain directly with your mind. The brain is your source of insight (hunches) and visualization (mental pictures). Use all of the brains priceless assets while playing Darts. For best results, train the brain well.

THE MIND is your knowing awareness. What you live with and use to make daily choices and manage your life. Use the mind to set up your body for the brain. Remember! The mind **IS** the master of the brain!

MAY YOUR DARTS ALWAYS BE STRAIGHT AND TRUE.
BEST OF LUCK AND KEEP SMILING!

BUDDY

INTRODUCTION:

Many believe Darts (today) is the world's fastest growing indoor sport. Yet, until now, players saw few 'how to' facts. Books focused mainly on dart history, the game's stars, world records, other games, rules, etc. Dart players looking to improve their game, saw few clues.

"*WINNING DARTS*" takes an important step in filling the void for fans of a unique, exciting sport. The book will: Introduce you to winning Darts, help you play to the best of your abilities. It shows ways to hone needed skills with sound hands-on drills to spot and fix faults.

Most important, knowing the ropes, you can feel and act like a WINNER, no matter who throws the final dart. Love for the game and knowing you gave your best yields this outlook.

USING "WINNING DARTS":

The book contains a wealth of facts! The articles are PURPOSELY not in a set order. Trying to grasp all the points in a single reading would surely frustrate you. Skim over the articles, picking one you feel may best help. Stick with a helpful idea until you find the best way (for you), forming a habit. Learning how, forget you know. Then, go back for more. Like a treasure hunt, dig out the nuggets for a better game.

A few BASIC points run throughout the book, but each article paints part of the whole picture. Some articles DO clash. What works for you may not for another player. Stick with one point at a time. After you make any change, retest all ideas tried before without luck. A change may need a further one(s) for best results. A hint or two may improve your game so much that you become a fine player. Look at your game as an uncut diamond; polish every facet until it sparkles.

Follow this program and you WILL improve, perhaps a great deal. At the very least, you gain much more pleasure from playing and watching others. Darts is truly a sport in which the "good guys and women" do win. Darts is everyone's sport. Disabled players too, even the blind, gain a great deal of joy playing Darts.

COMBINED INDEX AND TABLE OF CONTENTS

ARTICLES 1 to 80

COMBINED INDEX AND TABLE OF CONTENTS

ARTICLES 81 to 152

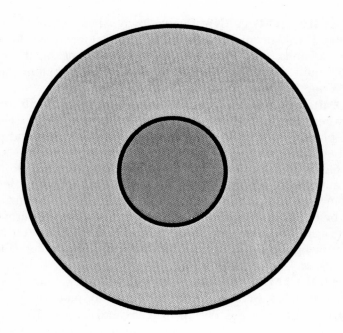

The *lucky* darter

Lets their brain control the throw.
Uses their mind and skills wisely.
Controls their emotions.
Keeps the body still using only their arm.
You are in charge do not blame others.

ACHES AND PAINS: Begin slowly when starting to play Darts, or after a long break. Go cautiously, in $\boxed{1}$ short sessions, then extend in steps. Never jump in, throwing darts until sore. You will throw many darts before easily delivering for long periods.

Darts is a complex physical and mental sport. Small aches, anywhere on the body, may distract shooters from their game. Yet, players with total mind control can turn off pain and play well. At times, veteran dartists do play with pain.

Get a doctor's okay before playing with pain, despite how big any match. Think! You could turn some minor ache into a chronic disability. Throwing with pain, you soon know if making it worse. Think long and hard before risking never throwing Darts again! Practice with your off-hand (see article 100) instead of throwing with brief soreness in wrist, arm or shoulder. If pain persists, seek professional help.

ADJUSTMENTS: Analyze games after, not during, matches. Scrutiny is one big reason for practice. $\boxed{2}$ Focus on game tactics during matches, not basics! Train your brain well, in practice. It sees you through without help during a match. Let the brain act!

Be aware! At some point in every darter's career, they will likely need to make major changes in methods and level of play. I recently reached such a point. Poor circulation made my hands and wrists too stiff to use my normal grip and delivery style. After years of using the catapult then a wrist shot, I now throw with my wrist stiff. This way is not as good though and I may also have to move down. At least I can play!

Do not be stubborn by refusing to adjust or move lower. You will hurt yourself and your mates. Darts is just as thrilling at any skill level. Every perfect throw and win is still a joy. You will quickly fit in with other fellow darters. No one will look down on you, but respect your making a hard decision. Failing to adjust, you face much frustration and anger. Better to quit!

$\boxed{3}$ **ADVICE:** Ask for help! Welcome all comments from others. Many will gladly help. How else can you

$\boxed{\textit{Mike McGonicle}}$

improve once mastering the basics? Another darter may see what is holding you at your present skill level. Would you not like to know also?

Respect all sincere guidance coming your way from partners, rivals, observers, anyone! Ignoring advice may cost you many games and slow your progress.

A big note of CAUTION here! No one knows or can tell another player HOW to play Darts. Pros putting on shows, without fail, hear such questions as: "How can I get better? Is this the best way? What is your advice?" Small wonder pros keep giving exhibits! Were improving so simple, we could all become pros by simply asking questions. Growth is hard work!

The honest answer to most requests is, "I truly do not know." As often stated in this book, no one plays Darts like another. We are all unique! Others may merely point out what works in their case. True, pros may mention clear faults, as using one's wrong hand, throwing underhand or other equally 'foolish' methods. She may err in pointing out some 'errors' seeing the odd styles used by many fine dart players.

Share knowledge (tactfully) with other darters, friend or opponent. They may in return, point out faults in your throw. Spotting small throwing errors is much easier with help. Welcome any aid in spotting flaws. We all want to improve to play at our best skill level. Becoming upset and ignoring help is taking the long road toward playing your best.

If all play better, Darts will become more exciting, leading more people to seriously taking up the sport. Darts would then become more popular, earning future entry into The Olympic Games. TV will rapidly advance and spread a great sport worldwide.

AIMING: You cannot aim darts like a gun. NO precise method guarantees hitting a target. Align your dart, guided by past results.

4

A great aiming method for a new player is as follows: Raise your upper arm level with its shoulder. Keeping forearm vertical, locate the target through your thumb. Then, focus on the target, throwing once your mind clears. Note! Tall players often need a lower point.

You may need to swing your arm sideways while keeping the forearm vertical. Reaching an ideal spot may mean bending at the waist (to-or-fro), but not as far as to lose your balance. At first, setting up can feel awkward, but is soon a habit.

Avoid lowering your upper arm. Comfortably keeping your arm as high as possible is the secret to locking your elbow in place. How steadily you hold the elbow decides your control over a throw. Bobbing elbows cause shots to stray all over the board or wall.

Two cautions. First, avoid forcing your forearm into position. The final forearm position should be one you can repeat with little (or no) thought. Second, take care not to hold the arm TOO HIGH. Throwing downhill, gravity becomes a big problem. You are throwing on your arms downswing, and the dart's arc.

What is this stance's logic? It forces darts into a straight line from the eye to target. Any other pose burdens the brain, as it must adjust for where the dart would otherwise hit. Throwing from any other spot includes some angle.

Delivering off-line darts, skilled dartists adjust for angles from habit. Try this straight-ahead method, checking results. Do not feel you MUST alter an already effective aiming routine.

Some darters cannot use a straight-ahead approach safely as darts come dangerously near their eye, on the backswing. Cures? Use a shorter shaft, flight or both. Yet, these changes may upset your dart's arc.

To avoid injury, bring the dart back beside your head at eye level. The dart should ideally stay within view. Do not purposely watch dart or hand, but avoid losing sight of them. The brain has only an instant to adjust as they reappear.

Your brain is a fantastic device, correcting for most faults. Yet, do not overload your brain with loose ends, let it focus on the more vital details.

Paul Brodeur (PUDGE)

Tinker with starting arm positions until finding what works well. Then, stay with those results. Note how a dart arcs as your arm pivots at the elbow. Ideally, starting with your arm vertical is best, but may not work well for many reason(s), mental or physical. Most dartists align shots guided by a spot on their hand, arm or dart, knowingly or not.

Go through a normal setup with your arm, and then bring it back several inches. Notice how your aiming spot is then above or below its first point on the board. The arm's arcing is why. Arcing is no problem if starting at the same spot each time, even with the arm crooked. Always release your dart at the same point in its arc, ideally at the top. Even with a perfect release, ignoring your arms position can mean a miss.

Arcing is more crucial using the catapult throw. Wrist throws lessen your arms motion and the dart's arc.

AIR MOVEMENTS: Stay alert for air problems. Note heating and A/C ducts and returns. Watch for hot light bulbs. Suspect all air moving items. They may divert perfect throws.

Bulbs create easily missed hot spots. Hot spots cause darts to hop in their path. Hot air is thinner, not supporting dart flights like room air. Watch closely to see the dart do a little jig through hot air pockets.

Often, you cannot fix air-related problems. Show courtesy, make all shooters aware of air movements. See how serious this problem is for you by throwing darts outdoors on a breezy day.

ALCOHOL: Linked by its pub setting, alcohol is the most sensitive Darts issue. Money for supporting dart leagues, dart events and sponsoring players comes mainly from the liquor industry. Their backing helped Darts reach its present state.

You should not object to others drinking during play, if no one suffers in any way. A few drinks may improve (or hinder) a player's skill, depending on the person.

Using a night of Darts as an excuse for acting foul cannot make you a team asset. In excess, alcohol ruins darting skills and

Jon Simonelli

you look, at best, foolish. You could create a real hazard for others. Better darters never humor such people. Think of your team image.

7 **ARC:** Visualize your dart's arc as you throw. Ignoring this arc could cause problems as you progress, or fail to do so.

Throwing a dart without an arc is impossible! The problem with trying for a perfectly flat flight path is one of control. Avoid excess force. A dart's arc is flatter when thrown easier.

Go with the dart's tendency to bow in flight. Work instead on improving rhythm, grip, follow-through and release. Fine-tuning skills, darts fly with a minimum arc, for your style.

Place your dart into a slight upward curve. Also, avoid releasing on hand's downswing. Seldom seen today, out-of-style feathered wooden models arced much more than today's tungsten darts. High looping arcs are hard to control and throw with accuracy.

Remember; different arcs give unlike results. Small changes in your grip, release, or follow-through may improve the dart's arc. Target distances can vary by several inches. A dart can drop a lot in one inch. Big arcs make the path longer and see more gravity pull.

You could try placing a long mirror to one side to watch your dart's arc. However, the motion is hard to detect. Best to have someone watching as you throw.

ATTITUDE: In throwing darts, maintain a steady mental outlook. For example, do not fool around in practice and be dead serious in matches. Think of your **8** brain as a computer. "Garbage in = garbage out" is a computer fact.

Change an AMATEUR into a MATURE player. How! Drop bad *Attitudes* and place your *Ego* last. Get lucky. Work hard! Attitude is luck's mother!

Days do come when you feel staying in bed was truly your best choice. Even pros suffer those days! Upset to the point you

Cathy (Barry) Cedar	*Mike Cedar*

feel angry, force a smile. Look forward (and back) on better days.

◄ 8 Saying 'stay calm' is easy, doing so **HARD**. I endure nights quitting seems a good option. Do not let tough times bother you! Accept your lows. The game's high points far outweigh a few blue days. Recall those games you could seemingly win with both eyes shut.

Deliver every dart with a constant level of purpose, despite how vital any throw may or may not seem. Staying uniform is a vital dart strategy, steadying you during big matches.

Stay calm after all missed shots. Letting, say three ones in a row upset you could hurt by spoiling every later throw. Instead, use a miss to harden your resolve and focus on scoring better.

Playing Darts in a uniform mood lessens chances of loading your brain with faulty programs. For self-control, each phase of your dart game must remain identical every time you throw. Staying in control is harder for your brain if you fail to maintain evenness.

Think like a winner. Until you convince your mind, success eludes you. With 72, two darts in hand (and little time) do you play safe with a pair of 20's or 16's? A winner thinks. Double 16, Double 20 or Double 20 then Double 16. _**ANY**_ way he can win in two darts. Missing never enters their mind. Winners simply go for the win! True, combos like that are hard, and not made often (though more than you might guess). Trying a difficult out is superior to losing because of not trying. Going out on a hard shot combo, under pressure, is a great confidence booster.

A team may include many, or all, great players. It could win most or all matches while not earning the title GREAT. No team ever earns praise if one or more members harbor attitudes! Titles exist in peoples minds and not freely given to cocky players or teams.

AWARENESS: A skill needing improvement. Be aware of all bodily actions when throwing. Sense your **9** 'place in space' so the brain can sense oddities.

While enduring a serious problem of nerves, you may yet

Tom Dwyer

7

score well at Darts, by standing still. Swaying, tiptoeing, jerky throws and other poor habits can slip by an unaware mind. How can you fix a problem not knowing one exists?

Work at building calmness during practice, when usually more at ease. Once learned, stress cannot hide clumsy acts.

Strad Darts invented a sure-fire method for gaining awareness—see Article 112. Using this product is like having a dart tutor spotting *every* mistake, to build a solid stance and delivery.

10 **ELIMINATE BAD HABITS:** How quickly we pick up poor habits! Replace faulty habits with good ones. You can erase problems. Do this in practice.

As a habit, I once went up on tiptoes when throwing. I cured the problem using a better habit for a week. I kept both feet flat on the floor, gently locking my knees, throwing this way for an hour each day.

At first, I felt awkward and threw wildly. Paying no heed to where darts landed, I kept going. Three or four days later my game returned to its original state. Then, my game began improving, giving me motive never to go on tiptoes again.

Two other ways to stop body movements when you throw are: First, while seated, place your elbow and upper arm FLAT on a table, counter or other surface as if delivering a dart. Keep going through your entire delivery motion. Done often enough, you break the bond of putting your body into every throw. Second, lower the dartboard and throw while seated on a high swivel chair.

An unusual way to throw with no movement, in practice, is as follows: Stand so one or both shoe heels touch the ochre instead of the tips. Crazy, maybe! Yet, unless a contortionist, I doubt you move anything but your arm. An easier method is to shoot standing on either one leg or tiptoes. The mind, intent on balance, gives total control of delivering the dart to the brain. These steps quickly expose flaws.

BEFORE YOU THROW: Consider the result of hitting

$$\boxed{\textbf{\textit{Karl Ebert}}} \qquad \boxed{\textbf{\textit{Paul Kane}}}$$

your target. You can fix misses, but not thinking about $\boxed{11}$ hitting a target is unwise. Throwing without thought at a wedge will cost you many winnable games. Trying foolish shots, you cannot help leaving poor out combos or busting. You must be able to hit all doubles, but avoid those you rarely make!

An example: With 86 left, you throw your first dart at trip 20 hoping to leave 26 with a hit. Double 13 is 'your' out because you feel at ease there, often making the shot. Oops, you miss, hitting a single 20 leaving 66. Now, 'without thinking,' your second dart again goes at trip 20 — BINGO you score. You must now hit six (Double 3) to win with your last dart. THEN, you think DOUBLE THREE! I never made Double 3 in all my years of league play! Your rival, at 32, can make his shot.

You now have NO options and must go for Double 3. Although you may make this shot, the odds are slim. A better way! Go for Double 20 or trip 18 with your second shot. Double 20 leaves <u>your</u> 26. Trip 18 leaves 12. A great second choice, Double 6 is right below D13.

Do you see similar problems often? Start thinking before throwing. Do not fault others when losing matches by not thinking.

$\boxed{12}$ **BETWEEN TURNS:** What should you do while a rival shoots? Watching is wasted time, as you cannot (legally) influence his darts. Put breaks to use. Check scoring with the chalker *BEFORE* pulling darts. Is yours correct? You must spot errors, no one else.

Check your opponent's tally. Fix errors at once, while possible, notably those in your favor. By failing to point out a mistake, you never feel right about winning. I won a match once, hitting a wrong double. I missed this. He was not even in yet, but I felt awful.

Inspect darts after bounceouts, hitting a wire or anything strange. Ditto, look darts over when hitting another one, robin hooding or other mishaps. Did the dart(s) receive damage? Are shafts and flights unhurt? Is one or more points dull or burred? Is a flight in danger of falling off or a shaft loose? Try using

$\boxed{\textit{\textbf{Dave Harrington}}}$ $\boxed{\textit{\textbf{Jerry Aubin}}}$

9

SHAFTITE™—See BONUSES.

After examining scores and darts, check yourself. Are you tense, nervous or overconfident and not giving the game or team your best? Wake up and play 'smart' darts. Decide where to throw next turn.

Consider out shots when playing '01' games or best tactics playing CRICKET. A partner may resolve doubts. In team CRICKET, name a player to call strategy. Led by one mind, this eases the job for all. See CRICKET AIDS. Stay relaxed, comfortable, and throw normally. This only takes seconds. NOW, it is your turn!

BOLD: Never play defensive Darts! Meekness is a losing game. For instance, playing '01' games you must double out to win. With 122 left, you hit two ⟨13⟩ triple twenties. Now, you need a Double 1. What can you do? You seldom hit this double. Thinking such ideas, you are playing defensive Darts.

Here, you can play many mind games, like: "Why did I go for a second trip twenty? If I bust on Double 1, I waste two perfect darts, going back where I started. I didn't look ahead!" You could think many self-defeating thoughts. Still, you must deal with your next move. Facts do not change. Thinking negatively, you may as well throw that third dart on the floor. Hitting Double 1 now is unlikely.

A winner goes for the win without hesitation. WHY! She threw two perfect darts. Her mind will rarely be more on target. Waiting until her next turn (what is rivals' score), she may not get the chance. Later tries are not likely to put her more 'in the groove'.

Throwing the third dart away, do not become upset if your rival wins at their throw. Busting, going for Double 1 makes no difference now. Losing, trying a shot, you hold your head high.

BORING: Darters often use a lack of interest as an excuse for not practicing. Anyone short on ⟨14⟩ willpower may feel bored stiff. Should this be a problem, train with darters who think practice dull too.

Frank Iaconi	*Nancy Iaconi*

Play better darters, if possible. Playing easily beaten players, you learn little. Unless a tossup, you know whether you are the stronger or weaker player.

If the best darter, build the other player's skills quickly. You may own a knack for teaching or helping others. By helping those who will listen, you gain respect from all players. Watching and pointing out flaws in others' methods, you soon notice many useful pointers.

Lacking a teaching talent, work to become the ideal student. BOTH should learn new details in 'practice.' Avoid letting a session become a bout! Watch closely for another's flaws when working to better his game.

With one's skills under study, players must keep their minds open. Taking comments to heart, darters make no progress. Strive to help the other player to become the best dartist possible. In helping others, you too, learn more.

15 **BREATHING:** Often going unnoticed, the brain controls breathing. Notice how you now breathe. When throwing, breathing should normally cease. Double check, see that you do stop here. If not, train to breathe right. Focus on breathing patterns for a few practice periods.

Your arm moves up and down (a little, or a lot) when you breathe while throwing. Watching your elbow in a mirror, breathe deeply. See the movement? Best to throw after inhaling, when fresh oxygen charge's body and brain to peak form. If holding your breath distracts you throw after exhaling and fully relaxed.

When breathing stops, is not crucial. Doing so at the same point in your throw is. Learn to breathe correctly for a few sessions until it becomes a habit. Then, check breathing weekly.

BULLSEYE IMPROVEMENT METHODS: **16** The only way to hit bullseyes more often is throwing at them more. Any other system is the long way around. You alone decide how rigid your practice. Simply hit so many bulls' or plan a full-scale program. For example, throw bulls until hitting 50. Another method is a strict program of quantity and

Jim Carreau   **Doug Poisson**

time. Aim to hit 50 bulls in ten minutes. Reaching a goal, shorten the time element. Many avenues exist. Adopt one.

More bounceouts occur on bulls because so many wires merge there. For bullseye practice, I recommend counting a double bull ring bounceout as a single bull. After all, you placed your dart within the single bull area. You might remove an old board's center ring for bull practice. In matches, a bounceout, sadly enough, counts for nothing (except in Electronic Darts). If a stickler, ignore bounceouts. Stay constant, always using the same method.

You can use dozens of tricks for improving bull skills. Each player must find what works best. A few off-the-wall ideas: Use another dart set that you feel better with on bulls. Change grip or stance. Shut your eyes! (Really struggling, I score surprisingly well shooting blind). Move to one side or another. Back up a few inches. Watch the dart, not the board when throwing — YES, all mental ploys. Use any trick that works. Darts IS a mental game!

17 **CARRY:** Keep darts, extra flights, and shafts within easy reach. A few flight protectors may come in handy. Tote a sharpener for steel tip darts. Soft-tippers' need spare points.

Keep three other vital assets handy too: A warm smile, a sincere handshake and great love for Darts. A tip, gladly share your 'goodies' with friends and opponents. Rewards far outweigh this courtesy's cost.

18 **A CATAPULT:** A great likeness exists between a catapult and a well-thrown dart. The base of a catapult resembles your upper arm from shoulder to elbow. Its upright arm acts like your forearm. The cup, with its missile, models your hand holding a dart.

Catapults are very accurate weapons when well aimed by their crew or 'brain.' Load weight and arm tension staying true a catapult would hit its target (without wind) every shot.

When throwing darts, picture your arm working like a catapult. Keep the upper arm rigid and avoid swaying or jerky movements. Ideally, the forearm and hand should act as one. Do not throw with the wrist. Your wrist simply follows the forearm, straight ahead.

All energy should come from your triceps muscles, at the back of the upper arm. Avoid flexing any other muscles. Holding your forearm vertical, stay in a straight line over the upper arm before and during the throw. For uniform tension, bring your arm back to the same point every time before starting forward.

Throwing a dart faster flattens its arc. NOT HARDER! Do not try to control releasing the dart. Your brain handles the dart's release best unaided.

CELEBRATING: Hitting a double, triple or bull, rejoice! Hitting those targets is no small wonder. A

19

dart off track by a hair, at release, rarely hits the target. Thank your brain for its skills after making hard shots. Even new players can hit any target, with enough tries. Pros make difficult shots look easy.

The brain is your success secret. Your mind knows next to nothing about throwing a dart. Praise works wonders for one's ego and skills. You need not jump for joy after every scoring shot, but is okay after game winners. If not, a silent "YES" or "RIGHT ON" will do.

CEMENT FLOORS: These are hard on darts and players. Among other bothers, shafts and points break, damaged flights, lost flight protectors and loose

20

points. Bouncing darts get dull, burring rapidly. You too, tire faster from fatiguing feet and legs. If you cannot avoid playing on cement, use a sturdy rubber mat while shooting. Check darts often for damage.

21

CHALKING (DUTIES & RULES): As both servant and master, chalking (scoring) is an unusual job. Your duties include.

Keep the score for both sides.

Stay totally fair.

Tell both teams when making any change.

Tell the shooter his score, before he pulls the darts. Be sure he agrees. Ask players to repeat their scores or somehow show agreement. The scorer's word rules after a player pulls the darts.

◄21

Bob Drake (DUCK)

13

Unless told otherwise, show when a player doubles in playing some '01' games. I point my finger, as if playing cops and robbers. Announce scores loudly, so all may hear. Confirming a winning shot, declare 'game'. Double check! Saying 'game', all darts become final yet still subject to correction. Darts falling out after calling 'game' mean nothing. The same as a dart dropped taking it out still counts!

Should a dart seem in danger of dropping out, do not delay calling a game shot. Taking the same time to check, declare 'game' whether the shooter is a teammate or opponent. Remember that a game shot counts even if initially unseen or miscalled. Later throws (purposely or not) do not change the outcome.

Check for errors. A shooter IS responsible. Still, you will feel awful causing someone's loss. The player(s) may be unhappy with you, too. Minor slips become final once the wronged team or player throws again. Gross errors (100 or more) are correctable before a game shot. **NONE IS FIXABLE AFTER!**

You (normally) are the one person, other than a player's partner(s), who can talk with the shooter. Other than telling a shooter when in, the score or calling a game shot you may only answer a player(s) directly. She must ask for facts, never advise. You can neither offer nor tell her what to hit to win, merely the total left, as 26—NOT Double 13.

When a question arises, an error occurs or you get behind in scoring, STOP THE GAME! Settle all issues before going on with any match. Ditto, if questions or disputes come up you cannot answer or settle justly. Someone (a captain) should be there with the power to decide. Get a ruling before going on even if a player or team finishes under protest. Expect problems. Know how to handle them.

Remember. The darts DO decide any final word on scoring. All errors made or announced, including a game call, are subject to change by facts. The best reason never to pull darts too fast. Be safe, not sorry!

Billy Worters

If shooters can see you, avoid moving without good reason or looking at them. Face the scoreboard. Do not talk with or in any way distract a shooter. Do not cheer for or against any player(s). Circle all high scores—*__NEVER__* the low ones! Stay at your post, except in defense from a wild or angry shooter.

A player or team can ask for a new scorer, for any reason, or none at all. If you ignore rules, a losing player (or the team) can and should protest. Else, chaos would soon rule.

Cheating, by stepping over the line, claiming wedges or totals not hit, is rare in Darts. Part of scorers' job to catch. Chalking, give a player the benefit of a doubt. ONCE! Watch and score as seen after that. Anyone caught or suspected of cheating soon lack rivals. Never risk your honor.

A pamphlet is in print with complete chalker rules and duties. I failed to find a copy. Yet, the items above cover all main rules.

22 **CHALKING (KEEPING SCORE):** The chore too few dart players do. For unknown reasons, many players refuse this needed task. Some better darters even welcome weaker shooters who chalk willingly. Others often lose respect for dartists refusing to chalk. Ignoring this failing makes them losers.

Besides popularity, a great reason to chalk is to learn Darts. Scoring is surely the best, painless, way to pick up many finer points. You can compare two games, while not worrying about playing.

With no playing burden, you begin to see many small errors. Great shooters (pros as well) make mistakes in the heat of play. Seeing others' errors, you become more aware of your own faults.

Follow each shooter's game, guessing at every move. Should a player make another shot ask yourself WHY? Grasp their thinking—IF ANY. If not, ask why after a match. With tact, naturally!

CHANGES: Distrust any changes seeming to cause great results. Never make a change failing the test of time. Try new

Jim Stymiest

ways yet know they may prove to be poor habits in the long run.

A great rule, trimming is superior to adding. Test all changes at your practice board, never in matches. New ideas often cause startling gains simply because we focus on changes. We correctly turn all other actions over to our brain. The brain sparked those marked gains. Once adopting a new method, we return to old habits, trying to control darts with our mind. You should find better ways. Be very choosy!

OUTSHOT CHARTS: Remove or ignore charts. Charts represent guides, often poor choices for any one darter. Using charts exactly cramps one's style. Some tourneys ban their use. Then what can you do?

Think on your feet, knowing where your next dart should go without second thoughts. Stopping often to check suggested outs is a negative. Any pause upsets your rhythm, breaking your focus. Delaying often makes you appear and throw like a beginner. He who hesitates usually loses at Darts.

I strongly advise new players to ignore outside help during matches. You improve quicker using your own mind. Relying on charts may become a serious crutch. Give your dart game a big boost. Avoid charts!

Each dartist uses their own best way of reaching 'pet' doubles. Going for seldom hit outs is a losing move. How you get there, is not vital. We all hit certain numbers more easily than others. Throw at YOUR 'easy' wedges when possible.

Know right away where to throw that next dart! How! Like hitting bulls, work at each number until forming a habit. In practice work on one number at a time, say 25 or 31. Select numbers at random or in some set order. Mastering a number, check it off then work on the next. Once finishing all listed numbers, REPEAT. Find the safest and quickest combos (FOR YOU) to reach your best double(s). You learn much faster using a routine than random numbers.

I recommend starting on the odd numbers five to 99 (only one combo for 3). Example: With 5, you quickly learn whether to go

Tony Manzello Jr.

for 1, Double 2 or 3, Double 1. Once expert at low odd numbers, work on higher ones. Start low and work up to the bigger numbers. You learn faster because in matches you work toward the lower numbers. Straying into triple 16 trying for trip 19 with 89 (leaving 41), you will surely know your way from there. Know the math. It is essential!

Even numbers, generally, present fewer problems. Yet, know your strong and weak points. Unless necessary, avoid your poor numbers.

CLOTHING: Dress for comfort. Your attire should allow free body motion. Any hitch to smooth throws is a negative. Wear team shirts or uniforms to all matches. Visible IDs add greatly to team spirit. Shabby clothing reflects on you and your team.

COACHING: A BAD habit! Avoid giving shooters' orders, notably new players. Conduct (needed) coaching after matches, while slips remain fresh in a player's mind. Never, openly scold a darter! Coaching makes it hard to focus and give ones best! Some leagues penalize coaching with a lost game.

True, new players make many mistakes fatal to a game's outcome. Yet, few beginners progress any faster or, even as well, with someone hissing in their ears. A complex skill, throwing and playing Darts is hard enough. Coaching can make this task worse.

Nonstop coaching harms many players. Some may hurt or forever ruin their game. Darters can depend on help so badly they never reach their true potential. Like using crutches, depending on their help too long makes walking unaided one day harder. At some point, rookies must go on alone. No one can help.

New darters (veterans too) must know making boo boos is how we improve. Errors teach us to adjust and avoid repeats. We seldom learn from others' mistakes. Amateurs must make their own bloopers before seeing error(s) and moving forward.

Never allow anyone to coach you while shooting. You will

Campanale's Backroom Tavern

profit more making your own decisions. In team games, when unsure of best strategy, use a partner's wisdom. Backup help is one reason for a partner, but not as a crutch. Stand on your own two feet. Poise makes you a much better player.

27 **CONCEIT:** No serious dart player can afford pride's luxury. You cannot give the focus needed to win worrying about appearances. Think only about your play. Teams need shooters, not prima donnas! Fans watch the board, not you. Losing by ignoring the game in play, you need not worry about others watching. They WILL NOT! Yet, playing Darts is a low-cost way to build one's ego, a priceless gift.

28 **CONCENTRATION:** An intense focus is a great darting asset and one talent you must learn. Note how better dart players appear deaf. Honing one's focus is one reason pro's throw so much. They have sharp manual skills, but keep working on focusing abilities.

Practice Darts under many settings. Play a radio or stereo while throwing. Play programs like rock, soft music, talk shows or sports events, any you hold a keen interest in hearing. Place a TV set where its screen is visible, and then raise the volume slowly, in steps. Notice how intent you become. Once in the groove, you become oblivious to sounds and sights.

Throw in silence also. This upsets many players. Throw with a TV set on with no sound. Keep shooting until totally unaware of motion on the screen.

You hear many noises during matches. Block out confusion like the chalker or other games. Loud jukeboxes, yelling and spells of dead silence also occur. Stay at ease no matter what the distraction(s).

KEEP YOUR COOL: Control your emotions. **29** Instead of sympathy, anger repels others. Acting a martyr never works. In any match between equally skilled darters both get a 50 percent chance at winning (one in two), great odds I think. Losing ones cool in a bout can drop their odds of winning to one in ten. An uphill battle!

Increased odds of losing is a steep price for lacking self-

Billy Christie   **Grafton Crossing**

control. Upset, keep rage inside shielding it from others. Onlookers think anger childish.

Go with the 'flow.' Stay cool under fire. Self-control is a huge asset. Players win many games thought 'lost' simply by refusing to quit. A calm air can distract other players more than great darts. Trying to finish first puts added pressure on some players. Their tension may rise when the threat of losing appears not to bother you.

30 **CORENA:** An acronym for **CO**mfortable, **RE**laxed AND **NA**tural, vital guides for throwing great darts. Apply this checklist to all game facets, manual or mental. Forcing methods is never a positive move. Try new ideas, avoiding those not fitting CORENA's mold. Test many ideas to steadily improve.

Rule out no idea simply because it feels awkward at first. Make an honest try. Your brain quickly adjusts to helpful new methods. Yet, after a fair test period, stop using any system seeming to work wonders if you must think about or force actions. Another way must exist without breaking CORENA's rule.

31 **COUNTDOWN:** Make the following steps a habit. Never vary!

ONE, (Always): At the line, know what you want or must do, and then position feet and body. Keep an 'I intend to win' attitude.

TWO, (Always): Check your grip and dart positions are right. Set arm and wrist at your correct angle. Narrow vision (avoid blinking) to the target. Point your elbow at the target and line up the dart. Once ready mentally, hold your breath. Clear your mind and allow the brain total control. Visualize a perfect (scoring) arc and THROW the dart. Follow through by pointing your index finger at the target.

Unless a game ending shot, make no setup changes. Taking a deep breath, rate results. NEVER become upset! Decide the next shot. Repeat from STEP ONE, moving only the eyes if a new target.

Daniel Bolivar

32

COURTESY: At every match's end (win or lose) your first duty is shaking hands with a rival(s). Start a great habit, turn and offer your hand, at once, to console or to praise. Applaud great darts, <u>no matter who</u> throws them! Caution, expecting a handshake and getting a power slap can bruise. I know!

DO NOT rush to pull a winning dart, *unless* in danger of dislodging. Accept **NO** praise from others' first. The rudest Darts' act is turning your back on rival(s), to sulk or celebrate with others. As a runner-up when victors broke this basic rule, I vouch for the dismay.

Beware! Some darters become *EXTREMELY* fond of their darts. Unless you enjoy risky living, never use or handle another player's darts without first asking. Even generous dartists prefer you ask.

IN THE DARK: An unusual method is throwing with your eyes closed! Use this unique practice system for studying and improving one's game. Especially true when working on a wrist shot.

| 33 |

Start by aligning a shot as usual, and then close both your eyes when ready to throw. No matter how still you thought your body was its actual swaying may alarm you. Your sense of balance takes over when vision stops controlling the mind. You become keenly familiar with your inner sense of poise, our mind's so-called third eye or pilot.

Blind people continually depend on this sense while most others use it rarely. You must tap this skill when plunged into inky blackness without warning. You might face this problem in a power outage or when waking in pitch-blackness. Needing to move around or get to safety without lighting, you use this skill.

Once or twice, you may stub a toe. Yet, how well you navigate blindly is amazing. The brain 'sees' each item in your path with little effort. You often put your hand on a doorknob with one try. You can even set your foot on the center of a stair, sensing when reaching the last step. Truly a feat, as with eyes open we still watch the placement of our limbs.

| ◄33 |

Walter E. Ackerman Jr.   *Michelle L. Ackerman*

Stand with both eyes shut, ready to throw. If your body sways, stop movement by whatever means works. A few methods follow: First, relax your entire body. Then, shift your weight, moving feet, the opposite arm or both, twist or untwist at the waist.

You are on the right track when able to stand in place for a full five seconds. Open your eyes long enough to see if you must move the throwing hand. Repeat this action until rarely moving arm or hand. Body swaying is 'THE FLAW' keeping better shooters from getting beyond a certain skill level.

Once focused on not swaying, throw at the bull area. Note your reactions, a great way to detect and work toward erasing poor habits. Sense problems like arm, hand or wrist flurries, going on tiptoes or dipping. You will find it easy to sense all small movements. While throwing, notice your responses. Your body recoils if you throw too hard. Erase body flinching, it acts on the dart at release. Throw as if in slow motion.

A wise motto is "easy does it." Many darters disagree. Sadly, those players would benefit by easing up on their throw. Throwing a dart hard, not simply guiding it, requires added muscle. Throwing too fast or hard creates a 'trying to catch up with the dart' feeling. Your mind must focus more, too. Using extra muscles adds tension, increasing possible errors. The added focus needed also reduces your brain's control.

An easy dart throw does not cause a lower finish! Using a proper grip, throw easily, almost lazily. Darts, easily thrown, do finish higher, while also flying faster, smoother and more accurately. Satisfy doubts by testing an easy throw. Throwing easily, the brain adjusts quickly.

Now, throw your dart. Leave your arm extended with the finger(s) pointing at the board. Before you look, rate your throw. Did the motion feel right, with little body or arm movement or muscle tension? How close did the dart land? Did you sense the dart high, low, left, right or on the money? Listen to the sound as the dart impacts. Notice how the tone changes, when near or hitting the bull. Check your ratings after each throw. The brain

Linda Leary   Frank Pulsifer

soon knows, within a half inch, where the dart hit.

Wherever the dart landed, check that your forefinger ends pointing at it. Failing regularly to point at the dart means you must make changes. You may need to alter grip or style a little, or a lot, to achieve this every throw. Pointing correctly, is a crucial detail of playing better Darts. Once pointing true every time, work on the dart ending as sensed.

Use this blind system to fine-tune touch and sense your body's balance and movements. Occasionally use this method for an entire session. Throw at least three bulls with both eyes shut to start each practice. Using this method, darters often hit several bulls in one throw, lifting one's ego and poise.

Improving, you may frequently throw better darts with eyes shut than open. This should not shock you. You may soon score consecutive bulls, doubles or triples. Reaching this skill level, further refine your throw. Work at making every shot smooth, exactly like your last perfect throw. Notice details like heartbeat and breathing. Work then, to become even more stable and finally attain total stillness and awareness.

One other skill to aim for is holding your dart with minimum finger tension while staying in control. Reach for the dart simply resting on your fingers, in danger of dropping. Reduce wrist and arm motion until simply flipping the dart. Follow through fully though! Cut the force used in throwing darts to a minimum. Amazingly, we need little energy to throw darts with great skill and accuracy.

This method helps you ignore hand and arm in your field of vision. One less distraction! Keep working toward your goals. One day you will do great feats. With your inner dartists help earn the title <u>D'Artist.</u>

This article, stresses the skills needed for throwing great darts—not sight or might. The skills needed! Stay attuned to the body, keeping total faith in your darting abilities, talents displayed by all great dart players. Fully develop these skills for best results.

◀33

Focus on feelings when playing in a match, as with your

Tim Mosher

eyes shut. Results may dazzle you and others.

DART WEIGHT: As a rule, men should use a lighter dart than women do. A dart cannot reach its `34` best arc using excess muscle. Women throw easily, using more finesse. A slower dart loses energy sooner, often dipping before striking the board. This is why women lob.

Ideally, men should slow their arm speed, and use more finesse. A man's physique provides power to burn. He must learn control. She throws darts correctly, but needs extra weight to reduce lobbing. Adjusting, by throwing harder, hurts her fine touch. She should use a heavier dart to stay on course.

`35` **BRISTLE DARTBOARDS:** Buy the best affordable sisal fiber dartboard. Buying cheap boards is wasting money. Treat boards with care and receive months, possibly years, of pleasant use. Care for your board. Direct sunlight and moisture are taboo. Blunt or burred darts quickly shorten a board's life. With light daily use, rotate boards weekly. Turn boards every day with heavy usage.

Hang a dartboard 68 inches from its center to the floor. Tape or draw a toeline 93¼ inches from the board's face, not the wall. Hang securely as a falling board (around 13 pounds) can easily break a toe or foot. Dropped or placed roughly, boards can warp beyond repair.

If you truly cannot afford a dartboard, ask for one. Yes, ask! Go where darters play league Darts. Ask for one of their rejects. Sponsors use the best boards' sold. Replacing used ones often. Many places give away or toss boards with much use remaining. If necessary, offer a small sum for their best discards.

Some reject boards are in woeful shape. A few may be decent. Many sponsors swap all their boards regularly and some look almost new. You can probably get a board with, at worst, a 'dead' bull area that cannot hold darts. You can still `◄35` use such boards!

Buy a standard 7/16-inch flat washer at a hardware store. This washer should measure 1¼-inches wide with a half-inch

---

Dave Kender   **Jim Kender**

hole, the bull areas exact size. Now, make all the bullseyes needed. The board can serve you for years.

Center this washer in the larger single areas of all light colored wedges. The 20 wedge is always the darker color. Using a sharp #2 pencil, trace the washer's edges with care. Mark close to the washer keeping the right shape and size. Before removing, blacken its center area with a pencil or black marker. Voila, ten bulls!

Then, (in practice), simply move 6 inches left or right of your normal stance when needing bulls. You are looking at an excellent bull area copy. One added bonus is no wires for bounceouts. When needing any light colored single, you are now shooting at a 'bull.' Repeatedly throwing at bull-shaped areas quickly erases the idea you cannot hit bulls (Bullitis, or lots of bull). This will greatly extend the board's life. You should now go right at bulls in matches.

NEEDED IMPROVEMENTS: Bristle board centers should be easily replaceable when no longer usable. (The first company offering this feature gets my business—for life!) Why not a practice board WITHOUT wires and many bull areas? Similar boards should be easy to make. Boards are much too costly to replace often.

We send people to the moon, why can we not make dartboards that resist (See Article 38) bounceouts. Why must we use boards with wires? A refined sport such as Darts could draft simple, fair rules for line shot scoring. Why make the sport overly hard?

Shooters get no break when their darts bounce off double, triple or bull wires. With the skill to come so near a target, darters surely deserve SOME score. This happened to me: I threw six darts needing two bulls to win a CRICKET match. My first dart bounced off the single bull's ring. The next **FIVE** ALL

◄35 bounced off the double bull ring! My rivals, using nine darts, finally hit a bull to win. The winners (though thankful) felt it an undeserved game. What could anyone do?

Chris Brown   *Ray Devoe (RAY-RAY)*

Mishaps upset all players, new or expert. Bounceouts is one big reason Electronic Darts is becoming so popular. An electronic board is set 2¾ inches farther away. Yet, darts not staying in do count. You get what you hit!

I consider myself a diehard steel-tip player—throwing nothing else since early 1985. However, if a soft-tip Dart league formed locally, a switch would tempt me.

When anti bounce darts came out, I stood first in line to try out this new idea, at hefty prices. Money presented no hurdle for me, IF I could reduce bounceouts. To date, I tried every model with little success. Even today, I regard my practice sessions as deep-knee-bend exercises. I spend far too much time picking my darts off the floor. I must play on a cement floor and must replace my dart points twice a year.

True, I see fewer bounceouts now than when I threw fixed-tip darts. Yet, I feel the improvement fails to justify their cost and upkeep. Price is not my gripe. I would pay more IF they worked well!

How crucial is this point? Unless solved soon, I fear steel-tip Darts may suffer and fade away!

HINTS: Use thumbtacks or push pins as markers, on a bristle board, when halting a game or practice session. For instance, use one if you must stop when doubling around in practice. Upon returning, you can see where to pick up, assuring equal practice on all doubles. Keep a few markers nearby, in varied colors, as useful in other ways. Quickly improve your math skills by removing the board's scoring ring in practice.

THE DARTS: A dart set must match very closely in weight. Your brain cannot adapt for uneven weights. | 36 |
Another vital point! Keep darts clean for a uniform feel and easy release. Wash darts carefully with soap and water often. Dry well, to remove any trace of dirt or soap films. CAUTION!

| ◀36 | Do not dunk movable point darts. Dipping this type of dart, take them apart and dry fully to prevent rusting.

Beware! Should you deeply bury a dart in the board (or a wall), remove with a pair of pliers. Grasping its point, work

Billy Pantazis

the dart out with care. Pulled by the body, a dart could lose its point.

Treat darts with care since they ARE precise tools. A bent point or shaft can alter its flight path. Check to see darts stay true by using flight protectors.

Pinch the dart in one hand at the extreme end of the point using thumb and forefinger. Then, place its flight protector against a finger of your other hand. Slowly spin the dart, watching its body. Wobbling shows an untrue dart. Inspect flights first, for flaws or damage, and carry spares.

If a new flight fails to correct a wobble, check the shaft. Straighten a metal shaft (gently) by hand. Shafts of another material may snap when bent. You lose nothing, as you should not throw darts with bent shafts. Keep extra shafts too.

If not stainless steel, you could possibly true a bent steel point by hand. Bend cautiously, enlarging a point's retaining hole could make it more oval than round. Then, even a new point may not be straight. NOTE! Applying too much side pressure can damage anti bounce points.

Make sure darts fit your hand. Forcing hands to fit the dart is a big mistake! Some players must even consider the dart's thickness. Forced grips are never comfortable, natural or relaxed. Never break the CORENA rule!

A tungsten dart's balance point is sensitive. Place the thumb a bit behind its balance point. Move your grip back if the dart flops or ends with its tail much higher than the point. Shorter shafts or flights with a smaller area may help. If flights hang down, move your grip forward, test flights with more area or longer shafts.

DART BARREL LENGTH: Use a shorter dart with a two-finger grip and when beginning the delivery close to your body. With three or more fingers on the dart, or starting farther from the body, use a longer barrel. A dart's length is relative. One you think short another may think long. Test a variety of darts. Do not quickly choose a set. Every darter's needs differ.

Tungsten darts are thinner, smoother than brass or nickel and

Bob Mitchell   *Billy Drohan*

much harder to hold and control. Knurling and grooves do give a better grip.

DELIVERY: The fastest, least guided, part of your dart game. Finish with forefinger pointing at the [37] target. Follow through by fully opening the thumb and fingers. You can do little else. Yet, avoid feeling any tension in your forearm.

Due to its complexity, leave the entire delivery motion to your brain. Set feet, body, head, and arm in position. Checking grip, hand and dart placements simply give your brain control. Use your mind well when setting up the body; this lightens the load for the brain. Maintain a firm belief that the brain knows exactly how to hit all targets. Then turn that inner computer loose.

With total faith and perfect setup, you would always throw perfect darts. Darts is truly a thinking-man's sport until the actual delivery. Then, the brain is in charge. Never stop improving your physical methods.

[38] **DEGREES OF DIFFICULTY:** As one gets better at Darts, the game becomes harder. Teams rely on their better shooters more, increasing the pressure. Great players block out this burden.

Throwing tight groups can work against you by blocking targets. A miss, at the 20, means a 1 or triple 5 at best. Unskilled darters, missing the 20 wedge, often stray into triple 12 or 18.

Darts do bounce out more often on better players from hitting wires. Great players see more shots go astray from hitting the body or flight of darts in the board. Robin hooding, as well, is more common. When these nuisances start happening, take heart. You are improving!

Steel-tip dart players cannot avoid the dart-bouncing curse. Bounceouts occur often as you improve and the better your rival the more a miss hurts. Until dart and board makers come up with answers, you should try anything to avoid these problems. Erasing one shot in a match could mean winning instead of losing.

Randy Maus   **Cheryl Maus**

Using anti bounce darts is a positive step. These darts cost more, needing extra upkeep. A few rare leagues may ban their use.

Extra sharp dart points will bounce out more often as they can dig into a wire's entire surface area. Lightly blunted darts reduce rejects by sliding more easily over wires with only dead center hits flying back.

New wireless boards, and those with special wires, reduce bounceouts greatly. Special boards cost more and are seldom seen in league play. These modern boards do give hope of solving a major headache.

The new BANDIT™ board has no wires, but very thin embedded bands of tempered steel. To introduce this board, I donated one where I play. Teams resisted the BANDIT™ at first, but then pulled rank to use it. Bounceouts are very rare with thus board.

DIPPING: Does your dart lose its zip, dipping downward right before reaching the board? Try **39** throwing from three to six inches behind the line. Throw that way for a few minutes each practice session, slowly building muscles needed to lick this problem. Take care, and avoid overdoing. Straining a muscle is easy.

A dart's dipping might mean you throw too hard or steer with fingers or wrist. If you see no improvement after a half dozen or so sessions, one or the other of these reasons is likely the problem.

DISTRACTIONS: Zoom in on the target as you **40** prepare to deliver a dart. Do not tolerate distractions. Meeting with problems, STOP! Fix any bother. Ask that a nuisance cease. If an intrusion continues, protest! Do so at once! Do not delay.

Throwing darts without obstacles is your right. Well-run leagues will uphold this protest, awarding you the match despite its outcome.

When the scorer does ANYTHING to distract or annoy you, say so. No chalker is a mind reader! A teammate could not bear

Tim O'Day

gum chewing by the scorer. The first time I scored for him he spoke up, after losing the match. I told him to let me know from then on, as it was a habit. After that, he subtly brought me an ashtray for my deposit. Yet, refusing to score, do not be too quick to criticize those that do.

41 **DO YOU BELONG?** Luckily, most people who should not play Darts display no interest in the sport. You may (rarely) run across this type. I met one in my years of playing. One too many!

He lasted a year (two seasons) in league play. Pleasant enough away from the board, he became Mr. Hyde at the line.

Meeting a griper, you know what I mean. They can find nothing right with the game or its players, nit-picking every detail. Such darters drain away all joy in playing. After five minutes, a pleasant night of Darts becomes a nightmare. These people are rushing headlong toward an ulcer, breakdown, stroke or heart attack. If you take after this type player, change your ways or quit! Darts is a hard sport played by imperfect people—period! Lighten up. Constant moaning or bellyaching (quickly) sets you apart from other players. Rough times lie ahead for you! Mates will make excuses only so long before asking you to leave. Foes also miss no chance to rub it in when you lose or make a mistake. You then fear losing and will no longer enjoy Darts. If unable to change, for health and happiness quit.

Playing Darts for any reason except friends or pleasure, win or lose, is crazy. Playing Darts well should be a challenge, not an ordeal.

DOUBLE ONE (D-1): Needing to hit D-1 often turns first class shooters into beginners. Fearing Double **42** 1, you finish there regularly. Know you can hit D-1 and rarely shoot at it.

Perhaps their problem is a fear of shooting low and busting. Many dartists moan, "I can't hit D-1." Thinking that way, of course, many CANNOT.

The best weapon to add to your arsenal is the ability to hit D-1 when needed. You will 'steal' more games with that one skill

Alan Dion (AL)

than all others combined. In practice, make a point of hitting D-1 often, perhaps starting and ending each practice session with a D-1.

Hitting any double several times increases your confidence. How is it darters do well on Double 20 or 18, on each side of D-1? Surely, players know after a miss going on to another double is possible, not with Double 1, though.

Conquer this mental block on Double 1 by 'walking your darts in,' shooting at a spot ¼ inch above D-1 with shots' one and two. You may make the shot with those first two darts. If not, go right at the double with your third dart. You are now well on your way to beating this crippling fault.

Do not totally avoid Double 1 or **ANY** other target, as you risk not being able to hit any number, fearing the next. A domino effect results. You avoid the number before the lead-in to the dreaded one, etc.

43   **EFFORT:** Give your best every time you play, even with weaker players. You cannot mask a lack of effort letting another player(s) win for whatever reason. Darters, sensing what is going on, feel betrayed. Think! You will also. If any player gives less than their best, all darters in a match feel cheated.

44   **THE RULE OF EIGHT:** Every dart player must know about this essential and useful tool. Throw at the triple 16, triple 8 areas with scores divisible by eight, from 96 down to 56.

Hitting a triple, you may reach 32 or 40, in one or two darts, possibly winning with two or three. With 48 left, go for single 8 or 16 to reach 32 or 40. If needed, use the first dart to reach those friendly numbers.

45   **EMOTION:** *Thinking* positive thoughts may win a few dart games. Yet, correct motion is the reason for most wins. *Negative* emotion causes many losses. Erase the E from Emotion. Instead, polish Darts throwing motion. Dump doubtful ideas and hurts.

START AT THE END: Every dart player wants   **46**

Bruce Burkholder

to throw better darts, even pros. Only a fool claims he knows all the answers because no two players throw darts alike. Two pros with sharply opposing methods, both throw near-perfect darts. How! All players use the skills' born with and practice.

Expert players agree, how you get there is not crucial, but getting there in the best way FOR YOU is. There, meaning to place your darts in an ideal path toward the target. Dartists are rare who display natural form, setting up and throwing perfect darts with no thought.

ALL better darters share a final hand and arm position after throwing. Common sense (often-uncommon) demands following through totally. Even simple flip shots need this for best results. A vital detail is finishing with your index finger pointing at the target. Until a habit, say "POINT" silently during every throw. To find YOUR ideal position, working back from a throw's end is an eye opener, when done correctly.

Start squarely facing the board with both feet touching the ochre. Now, place hand and arm where your follow-through ends after a normal throw. Extend your arm, pointing your index finger at the bullseye, like a pistol. Do not stretch! Stretching opposes the pointing method. Avoid over-extending the forearm. Going beyond the triceps contraction (about 45 degrees) raises the elbow. Vital! Simply reach for what is a comfortable, relaxed and natural, condition for you. Done wrong you cannot benefit. For now, ignore how you placed arm and hand.

With your index finger straight (not bent) and pointed at the double bull, look at your finger. Would a line down the index finger's full length, extend to hit the target? Note, I said the length of a finger not its tip alone. Ideally, if possible, you could look through your index finger's base then out its tip at the target. Like aiming a rifle, you must line up your finger's front

◀46 AND rear. Using only one sight, you cannot hit a target.

Place your index finger in this ideal ending position. You may need to make minor changes. Keep wrist and elbow as is! Simply rotate your entire arm at the shoulder. Be sure you sense

Jeff Walsh

no strain from shoulder to fingertips. Feeling no tension, bring your arm back slowly to a relaxed spot. Do not physically or mentally try to control this motion or its finish. For best results, you must do this motion naturally. Repeat, until finishing uniformly at both ends. This motion must feel RIGHT. Try the process with both eyes shut to ensure a natural motion.

Then, check your hand and forearm's new starting position and angle. Is this latest position how you now start your throw? Your forearm likely is now set at some angle other than up straight. You might think, "This will never work!" Yet, throw a few darts from that newfound spot. Your new stroke may feel more natural and need less effort. Kept up, you would soon note throws becoming truer, with tighter groups.

We all face the board in unlike ways when throwing darts. Many shooters feel uneasy or simply prefer another stance. Straight on feels clumsy for some darters. These players likely will find their arms at extreme angles using this newfound starting spot. A straight-ahead stance is awkward for many, making aiming hard. After forcing the arm upright, to aim, a darter must swing it back and forth. Their arm position can now seem unnatural. Small wonder some darters cannot shoot well from here.

Finding your ideal starting arm position facing the board, try the following. Keeping your forearm upright, do not influence it while slowly swinging the arm left and right. Note how your forearm's angle keeps changing from some extreme, to upright, or nearly so. That angle is rarely alike for any two players, as each owns a unique body build. The best angle with the board is where your arm comes closest to vertical.

A top U.S. pro told me he learned to keep his forearm vertical by using a wall as a guide. He placed his shoulder and elbow against a wall then went through his delivery motion often. He avoided touching the wall, coming only (brushing) close enough to sense it. Once a habit, he turned the duty over to his brain.

As said in other articles, an ideal may or may not help for

◄46

Mark Covotta

32

various reasons. You see great darters throw while holding forearms almost 45% with the floor. Some players would probably not throw well with arms upright. Yet! Changing **MIGHT** create a few new world class pros.

Learning to play, new players should work to hold their arms' vertical. Dart veterans, looking for ways to improve, should consider all the facts. However, avoid changing without a good reason.

Check your arm and hand placement every trip to the line until the position becomes natural. Make a habit of checking each detail. Your brain should catch any future, minor or major, changes in style or throw.

47 **EVENING OFF:** This is a touchy subject with some dartists. Players who practice evening off, most often 20's shooters, stay intent on keeping scores even, while far from a game shot. By habit, these players throw away dart after dart staying even. After a sane talk pointing out its pitfalls, few players listen.

Trying to prevent others from taking up the evening off practice too early, please consider. Doing well on 20, why go to the 19 or 17 to even up after a miss? Your mind is at ease with 20, why go to a distant spot for one throw. More often than not, you wind up missing. You may then score only four or five points with two or three darts.

Working the 17 or 19 wedge is wise IF hitting its triple leaves a possible out with one or two darts in hand. Scoring badly on 20's, your best option is usually 19. Really laboring, the 14 or 16 wedges may yield results. You need never fear evening off, with four odd numbers (7-19-3-17) side by side. A full one fifth of the board! Put off thinking about getting even until below 150 or even better 100.

Avoid this habit totally by scoring on the 19 wedge. Using that scoring area, you are always within one shot of even. Should you not score well on 19, return to the 20. By then, you may break a poor habit.

EXCUSES: Darts offers few defenses for poor

48

*Ray Gandolfo *A WINNER*

play! Rarely is a game area too hot, cold, damp, dry, noisy, quiet, light, dark, etc. Still, smoke-filled rooms bother some people. Tobacco smoke and a few other sticky issues can pose problems. Sensible players find answers. A badly lit board is unfair to darters used to proper lighting—bright, but without any glare or shadows. Playing with injuries can hurt.

We all throw under like conditions. A room may seem cozier to one darter than another. Players cannot let match settings bother their game. You must play as well away as at home.

No one can control luck. Throwing consistent darts, you should enjoy more good luck. Players throwing better darts are usually winners. Losing a match by a fluke or bad luck, forget it! Ill luck happens to all of us.

Dwelling on all your low points inflates what is going wrong. Soon thinking yourself unlucky, step one toward becoming so.

Make a point to practice daily if possible. Throw 'mental' darts when unable to drill. Go through the actual motions, if possible to keep physical and mental 'muscles' toned. How can you make excuses when rivals throw better darts? You must improve methods with daily practice and new ideas.

49 **DOMINANT EYE:** Most people's dominant eye is on their throwing hand's side. If yours is normal, you sense how people with opposite eye dominance manage when you throw darts off-handed.

Point a finger at the bullseye, closing first one eye alone then the other. Your dominant eye is open when the finger does not appear to move in relation to the bullseye. Neither eye is dominant when your finger moves with both eyes.

We normally aim a dart using our dominant eye, whether right, or left, or, with no dominance, centered. Aligning your hand with the other eye or centering between them may force the forearm from vertical.

You will see shooters who throw with forearms tilted at some angle. Many darters neglect faulty arm position while often throwing great darts. Their brain makes up for shifts from ideal

Donna Dennett   **_Scott Lucia_**

form. Yet, it cannot adjust totally.

To correct, move the elbow toward the center of your body, the head to one side, or both. In bad cases, alter stances to put forearm vertical.

One solution to this puzzle is as follows: First, focus on holding your forearm upright every throw, totally ignoring where darts' land. Work these changes until made habits so you need not think about each action.

Train to throw at targets without seeing your dart, hand or arm. Focus on the target you want to hit. Becoming upset makes for a difficult task, when darts stray. At first, your darts do wander badly.

Now, the critical point! You MUST keep shooting this way. Learn to throw darts again, like a rank beginner. Persist! You, in time, will notice progress in your throw's accuracy. Your brain is taking over the job you tried doing with the mind.

Take care! Do not slip back into poor habits. Rushing may cause a relapse. DO NOT! Keep checking that your arm is vertical as you look at the target. Follow this plan for a week or so. You will improve!

EYEGLASSES: Wear glasses, if needed, when playing Darts. Never let foolish pride prevent playing

| 50 |

your best game. How can you win without seeing the target? Watch for blind spots or mirages' eyeglass RX's may cause. Wear glasses in practice to see if they cause problems.

With problems, see an eye doctor. Tell your oculist. Ask if a change can correct problems. The doctor may fit you with special glasses to play Darts, as mine did.

| 51 |

RELEASE FAULTS: An early release results in darts sailing upward. Missing, the dart is more often high.

Fix this by placing your hand a few inches farther from your body before starting your delivery. A second method is shortening your arm's stroke.

On the other hand, a late release often finds darts landing low. Holding a dart too long could make it wind up with its flight (tail) end dipping down, at an awkward angle, or both.

Rick Brown (BROWNIE)

Correct late releases by placing your arm a few inches nearer the body when beginning your setup. A harder method is bringing your hand back a few inches more than normal.

Done before moving your arm, the first method, in both cases, requires little further care. Changing a stroke makes added work for your mind when throwing. Ideally, your mind should stay blank then.

If moving the arm proves hard, change your stroke. Work on changes when practicing. Done right, often enough, a new stroke becomes habit. Check for defects if darts wobble in flight.

Other reasons for steadily landing above or below the target. A rushed shot. Too much or little finger area placed on the dart or its top surface at release. You may throw too fast, hard or tilt your body. The front of a dart is too high or low at release. You release the dart early or late applying too much or little wrist action. A problem could mean faults, big or small.

FEELINGS: Throwing a perfect dart, you may experience unique feelings. Tune your mind to sense | 52 | any odd recurring emotions. Recreate these feelings, as well as is possible, as you throw. Simply knowing you threw a perfect dart you did exactly that.

FINESSE: Never overlook that Darts is a finesse sport. A fine touch becomes more critical as skills | 53 | improve and you compete with better players. Throwing darts hard makes control difficult.

FINGER MOVEMENT: Do your darts spin to the left, right, or rotate little or not at all? With excessive | 54 | spin, you twist fingers somehow at release. Spinning stabilizes a dart as its flight works to fly true.

This method is fine, when unable to correct poorly thrown darts in any other way. If able to throw a dart with no spin, twisting simply adds another complex action for your brain to handle.

Watch fingers closely when throwing darts. Other than a presetting motion, as when throwing a wrist shot, fingers should stay still.

Mike Tomczyk   *Bob Falvey (BUBBA)*

Darters may notice a finger(s) movement on (or off) the dart's surface. Reflex acts are normal and difficult to stop. Like throwing without backswing, the brain cannot do the impossible.

Presetting the wrist, fingers or both (like a wrist shot) may cut your stroke greatly. Then, use your wrist motion to fire the triceps (upper arm muscles) into action. Never try to throw from a dead start.

Use this method when unable to reduce or stop finger movement: Place fingers so that, after all reflex actions, each finishes correctly on (or off) the dart for your throw. Do not worry if unable to consciously stop finger movement(s).

Your brain may use finger movement to signal the triceps to contract. Efforts to anchor your finger(s) may result in other, more serious, problems. Try for control, but when your brain says NO, STOP!

Faulty finger placement greatly influences darts. At release, the dart's path should ideally need no help from its flight. A faulty throw makes the dart start tumbling in its arc. A dart's flight may or may not correct the arc before striking the board. If its balance is unstable in flight, a dart veers from the target. Keep trying small changes, during practice. You quickly know when hitting on better ways.

FINGER TENSION: Players often ignore grip
55 tension when looking for ways to improve. Keeping tension light avoids faulty finger action and its results. Yet, a grip must be secure enough for control.

One trick you might use is gently squeezing thumb and finger(s) on the dart before each throw. Then, simply let the fingers relax. The tensions left (or lack of, usually) in hand and arm should now work well, relaxing at the proper instant for a perfect throw.

The grooves formed in your thumb, fingers and the skin tension help achieve better dart control, without a tight grip. Try pinching the dart until proper finger tension becomes a natural part of your setup.

Your thumb supplies the force needed for throwing a dart.

Mark Russo (GUINEA)

Fingers stay in charge of accurate launches.

FINGER TEXTURE: We all possess uniquely shaped hands and fingers. Skin textures can vary from glass smooth to tree bark rough, on the same person. Medicated hand lotions can help immensely. You may need to consider how much your fingers sweat. Even a too-long fingernail may be critical when it rests on the dart.

56

Keep fingers uniformly dry where touching the dart. Moist fingers may stick, making a dart hard to throw smoothly. Use rosin or finger wax for sticky fingers. You could use ashes, chalk dust or dirt from a shoe sole in a pinch. These may help extra dry fingers too.

FINDING FLAWS: To grasp how difficult studying a dart throw is, when spotting problems— THINK. You are throwing a metal piece, weighing about an ounce (28 grams), at a target as narrow as 5/16-inch, 8 feet away. Flight time is 1/8 second while opposing gravity.

57

Throwing is merely the physical side of Darts. Experts say its mental side is 90%, or more! Nevertheless, players must build their physical skills first, before refining the other 90%.

Stay alert when helping fellow dartists' find weak spots. Watch for those 'little' details. Some answers may seem clear, though often not. Tiny flaws and faulty habits may creep into a darter's game. Defects can prove slippery. Watch basics to spot weak points.

Darters must stand unmoving, throwing smooth accurate shots with little effort and minimum motion. Dartists must carry out every part of their game easily, staying calm while playing naturally.

Watch from several spots: Stand behind the shooter, halfway between the ochre and dartboard, also (like a chalker) a step to the board's side. View throws from the left and right sides. Make mental or written notes. Have the player double around while studying form.

◄57

Watch for signs of undue stress, eye, head or body movement or a jerky delivery. Note if their throw is regular, well

Alex Yacyshyn (YAKA)

timed and rhythmic. Is she staying in focus and stable? Watch her dart's flight also.

Does the dart wobble? Does each dart show the same smooth arc? Watch the board, when using steel-tipped darts. Does each dart enter straight? Do the darts enter uniformly at the same angle and depth? Many faults could arise so stay alert.

Ask if she made any changes lately, big or small. Watch for progress as she works on (possible) flaws. In doing so check that a player does not pick up other poor habit(s).

With no visible physical problems, a darter may harbor a mental block. One remedy is sound daily practice. Two other possible cures are hypnotism, (may or may not last) and self-help cassettes. Strad Darts offers cassette tape information for relaxing before matches. See Coupon at back of book.

FLEXIBILITY: This is a mental asset used by better darters. How do you react when unable to hit a usually easy number? Facing control problems, move to another wedge (fast) until your touch returns. Unexpected things happen to all players. You will lose staying on a wedge with few hits. Shift wedges, when unable to score with five or six darts, if not too late.

58

Meeting this problem in practice, learn the other high wedge(s) where you score well. A backup target is vital when doubling in, without success, in '01' games. If your normal double fails you, move at once to your backup. Failing to adjust, you may be OUT before getting IN.

Do not resist changing. GO WITH CURRENT CYCLES OF YOUR GAME! What is your easiest double *NOW*? Do not be stubborn. Go for targets you can hit TODAY, but use common sense. Example: For years, I went in and out on Double 16, 95% of my '01' games. I could (and truly did) hit this double (in practice) with both eyes shut! Double 16 suddenly became just another number, losing too many games because I refused other doubles.

I then noticed, during practice, double 18 (my former backup double) was the easiest to hit. I started using it to double in with

John Ackerman   *Kevin Brown*

39

success. However, trying to go out on 18, I faced big problems. Hitting a single left me Double 9. To date, this double is my biggest block.

With no other wedge to shoot at, needing only bulls, for instance, note how you miss. Do most darts go astray uniformly, like an inch high to the left or low? If so, adjust your 'aiming' setup, mentally not manually. You confuse the brain with sudden setup changes.

With no clear pattern to misses try moving a little left or right at the line. Make a change quickly, while possible. In practice you have time to examine and correct problems. Not in a match!

59 **FLIGHTS:** Flights are a basic part of your dart assembly. Flights come in many materials, sizes, designs, surface textures and shapes. Rare players can throw darts without flights. All darters use them in a match.

You might test many flight types before finding the right ones. Changes in length, shape or weight of flights, shafts, or both can change your dart's path (for better or worse). Changing a dart's, shaft length, shape, or material, you may need a new flight type. Remember your method(s) also slowly change as you improve. Changes in style accumulate. Flights may, in time, no longer work well.

Use scissors to try out new shapes. However, use only new or pretested reshaped flights in matches. Old or reshaped flights are okay for practice. Some pros change flights after every game, a few every leg!

Feathered flights may give you an edge. While more easily damaged, feather flights rarely deflect shots or kick back. Feather flights cost more and are often hard to find. Most players favor the newer one-piece flight's strength and low cost.

Test a variety of materials. No other way exists to find flights right for your present setup. Going from hard to soft plastic or other fabric can cause small or big changes in a dart's arc and flight time. Each material reacts uniquely during flight to air resistance (drag). Surface textures (even of identical material)

Rich Renzoni

can alter a dart's fight too.

Saying all that, the truth is many darters see little effect between flights, including extreme changes. Some players notice a difference when their flights simply start fraying. No one can say why wild variations occur. Simply know flights can make a great difference.

Check flights often in matches. A damaged flight could divert your throws. Carry extras.

60 **FLIGHT SHAPES:** Used by most darters, Standard flights offer the largest area among the more common ones seen. A larger surface area gives added lift to a dart's tail. Flights with smaller area give less lift, but a faster dart. Kite, Teardrop, K2, VX and Slim (or Coal Crackers) are styles with small areas and including Standard's are the most popular. See FLIGHT PROFILES at end of book.

Other styles exist. For example, in favor with some English pros Bristol Whites are about 50 percent bigger than Standards. A larger area grabs air faster, allowing straight wobble-free darts. The Bristol style is not popular in America and hard to find. Its broad area is also the Bristol's flaw, deflecting darts and bouncing out more. Know that many other styles exist. You must look around for them, though.

A Standard flight's area is often not uniform. Style, only means a flight's general shape, not its total surface area, which can and does vary.

61 **GO WITH THE FLOW:** Teach the mind and brain to use your body's full range of motion. Forcing any body part is unnatural. Thinking about a motion, you are forcing your game. Make any needed changes for freedom's (BIG) bonus. YOUR body works like no one else's. Put your assets to peak use. Erasing all body tightness, in due time, cancels mental stress. Your body and mind are unique. Allow your brain full access to this dynamic duo! Consider the arm a direct branch of your brain, the dart a further addition. Giving your brain total control. It rarely fails you.

Darts is an ideal sport for applying Flow theory. 'FLOW,'

Dave Collins

41

means becoming so involved you ignore bodily motions and time. To earn the label 'Flow activity' a sport must impose set rules and goals. Challenge all your abilities. Allow players to adjust for skill levels. A game should also let a player know at once, how well he does and require a focused effort.

People with Flow profiles excel at Darts as they feel in control, win or lose. They can stretch skills to match events and set goals, know what they must do and quickly grasp and react to conditions. Such players focus well and are oblivious to time and outside turmoil. All factors needed to benefit from using Flow.

FOCUS: After buying a new dartboard, I dot all double and triple centers with an ink marker or a #2 [62] pencil. Then, when I shoot for a double or triple, I aim for my marks. Aiming at small targets within larger ones is a great way to build focus and tighten groups. Choose methods. Then, work on focusing.

FORM & DESIRE: Avoid form hang-ups! I [63] became a respected dartist in my league after playing two years. Then I figured by perfecting my delivery and form I could improve. I spent years chasing the ideal form. In hindsight, I see this quest was when my prolonged slump began. My darts and I looked great, while my game never improved.

Every match, someone told me how great my form was. However, I wished for an occasional cheer for winning a match. I went from winning 75 - 80 percent of my games to nearer 30 percent.

True, I now shot in a tougher league. Yet, I lacked some basic I could not seem to identify or regain.

Down deep, I thought my form was perfect, that results should come without really trying. My brain, though enjoying complete control, needed and expected more of an effort from me.

[◄63] I started watching better players more closely. At higher levels, I noticed how many darters still used what I thought awkward forms. Some were laughable, except for

Carol Houlihan

their winning ways.

A teammate throws a dart looking like a dying bird that ends hanging down badly. Yet, he has deadly accuracy. Should he make changes to improve how his throw looks? You tell him—I will never mention it!

What is desire? Desire is that little (BIG) extra inner drive making one stand out from the crowd. Rare is the person born with this trait. Luckily, you can build desire with hard work. Yet, perfect the details first.

The desire to win is more potent than form! Win your share of games by putting your all into every throw. Inner drive is your greatest asset.

Making this point clearer, consider how cars operate. Your body models a well-tuned auto. Both contain hundreds of complex parts working in harmony. A car's engine drives the whole works, enabling a vehicle to move. Your brain holds similar duties. Lastly and most important, BOTH need a mind in control to use those parts with skill. CONTROL is the key, mental (mind & brain) and physical.

Without a guiding mind, cars are simply piles of metal, no matter how modern. Despite how fit, a body is helpless without a mind in control. Your brain can move your body in many ways. Only your mind has the common sense to get out of harms way.

The world's best driver in the newest car is useless when careless. If a driver daydreams at the wheel, a simple pothole could ruin car and pilot. Owning ideal form and knowing all the tricks are not enough in Darts. Given time, anyone can learn the ropes. Desire gives winners an extra big edge. True, inner drive cannot ensure winning but lacking desire you are only another player. Desire also means 'HEART'.

THE FOUR F'S: (Firm, Fast, Flat and Follow) | 64 |
A solid base for throwing darts.

F1 = Firm: Grip a dart securely, while using no more pressure than needed for total control. Avoid holding darts with a death grip! Held too tightly, you cannot release a dart properly. Firm, means the throw too, deliver darts quickly, with authority.

43

Firmness results in smooth, crisp, accurate shots. Never throw a dart timidly or without full control.

F2 = FAST: This refers to the time it takes to deliver a dart and its time in flight. A straight, firm, well-thrown dart, using a proper grip, from a solid stance, results in a 'fast' dart. Flaws in any basic cause a dart to fly slower. A slow dart lets gravity work more and has a bigger drop.

NEVER adjust by throwing harder. Extra force totally ruins anyone's game. A delivery is 'fast' when the dart jumps from your hand, zipping smoothly to the board.

F3 = Flat: When a dart is 'fast' and 'firm'ly thrown the result is a dart with a minimum arc. Throwing a 'flat' dart does away with extra details. Your brain may now focus on other, more vital, facets.

F4 = Follow: A detail many darters ignore is following through with hand and arm, after releasing the dart. Finish with your throwing hand's forefinger pointing at the target. Focus on pointing in practice until it becomes a habit. With other methods correct, pointing makes a great 'aiming' device. Done right, pointing gives your brain a final chance to catch and adapt for small delivery errors.

GAMES: CRICKET, 301 and 501 are the three basic

65

games' new players must learn. These games are so simple you can learn their ABC's in a few minutes. Many other games exist, but are never seen in league play. I could fill 20 or 30 pages showing you how to play dozens of novel, often enjoyable games.

Yet, this book's aim is not detailing odd games and I doubt why you are reading. Other books teach many popular and odd games. Yet, knowing unusual games is useless if not played locally. You might introduce one or more new games. Yet, most darters' hands remain full mastering the big three—a lifetime task. I omitted space hogging cartoons and snappy one-liners too.

ALL dart games require a mix of manual and mental skills along with old-fashioned luck. Practice WINNING DARTS to play any game well.

VALUABLE PRACTICE GAMES: The game of 101 (straight on, double out) is great for darters with outshot woes. Many dart players see sorrow in

that regard, no shame in this. However, ignoring a weakness IS a great mistake. A big obstacle to playing winning Darts is stopping often to figure where your next dart should go. Learn Dart math by heart!

I saw an average darter blow a shot at a once-in-a-lifetime perfect 301 game—a rare feat, even by pros. Between so-so losing games he started 32, 60, 60, 60 – leaving 89. Without thinking, he went for the 20 wedge. Trip 19 double 16 was the ideal finish. Others are possible, but you must begin with an odd triple. He just did win the leg. Again, know your numbers!

Playing 101 trains you to avoid breaks in your tempo. Think quickly on your feet and know how to get rapidly and safely to the double(s) you often hit under pressure. Keep in mind that your opponent is always a threat. A game is winnable in two darts. Hit triple 17 double bull—hard, but possible (I've done it).

Develop several other valuable skills playing 101. Learn to use the Rule of Eight and hitting vital low odd numbers as needed. Namely 1, 3, 5, 7 & 9. Work the four wedges, 7-19-3-17, (at board's bottom) to go at once from odd numbers to makeable doubles. Hone your skill at going out on Double 1 and Double bull.

'TRIPLE CRICKET' (my son-in-law's invention) is a game that helps build several pivotal talents. Play TRIPLE CRICKET like regular CRICKET, but the scoring area stays within the outer triple wire. A dart landing outside this wire is a miss, not scoring. A variation is doubles are okay if called before throwing.

TRIPLE CRICKET's smaller scoring area forces you to group darts tightly. It stresses the value of going for triples, now a larger part of the scoring area. Singles now are nearly as hard as triples. Focusing on the triples will prove more

fruitful.

Results, you take more care with each dart, using

Scott Lemerise   **Sue Erickson**

finesse to greater benefit. Now, when playing regular CRICKET, full wedges look BIG!

Without doubt, games played with another dartist(s) are superior to playing alone. Lacking rivalry should not stop you. Use these games to improve your skills.

NEVER QUIT: Never count opponent(s) or yourself out of any match. No lead is ever a lock in this amazing sport. | 67 |

No matter how well a rival may score; she must throw the winning dart to end the match. The last dart thrown is the winner, not the first or biggest scores. In Darts, players come back every day to win games thought beyond hope. Skilled shooters needing 'just' a double or a bull to win, often, cannot hit the game shot. Think this could never happen to you? It will!

When practicing doubles, do you sometimes fail at hitting one? Do you give up and move on when faced with such problems? DO NOT! Stay in there. No matter how long it takes. If you must, carry over into your next practice. Harden your resolve to beat problems. You will see many.

When doubles' problems occur in matches or practice, simply relax. The worst reply is trying harder. Stay calm. Relax and deliver naturally.

Imagine standing aside in your mind, like an impartial observer. Make a frank judgment of your play. Do you lunge, lean, tiptoe, etc.?

GOALS: Develop daily and long term aims. How else can you tell whether your progressing. Such goals | 68 | are doubling around in less than X number of darts or finishing '01' or CRICKET games in fewer darts. Reaching a goal, make your next one harder.

| 69 | **GRAVITY—NATURE'S:** Never fight gravity. Use it! Shoot high, adjusting for any drop is much easier! Trying to throw darts with little or no arc could cause pain from a sore elbow. Stay at ease, act natural and relax with every phase of your dart game.

| 70 | **GRAVITY—YOURS:** No game is worth a stroke or

Madigan's Again

ulcer. Relax! Enjoy yourself when playing Darts. Stress could easily ruin your game. Stay cheerful to enjoy playing in or watching Darts more.

Reaching a high skill level requires a calm state of mind. Do not become wrapped up in your dart games. All dart players, including pros, endure losing. Accept losing, to become a better player.

GRIP: Your finger placement on the dart, is your [71] grip. A solid grip lets you throw straight, true, darts smoothly. Like all other facets of Darts, no one 'right' method suits every dartist. Grips vary greatly. One top player holds her dart at its point with two fingers. Other experts use three, four or all five fingers. Each shooter must work at finding their best grip. Your grip must feel comfortable and natural for a controlled throw. This lets you totally relax. Pinching a dart with fingertips and thumb gives maximum control.

You should not need to twist fingers for a usable grip. Luckily, most darters settle on a sound grip, near their first trial run, with little change of thumb and fingers. Yet, changing a dart's weight or shape, you may need to alter your grip.

While you improve, minor and often big, style changes may occur. Changes take place because your build and muscle tone varies with use and aging. Once your darting skills mature, finesse beats brawn.

No one grip is ever perfect or final for a dartist. You can only gauge your grip's accuracy by results.

GRIP CHECKS: Use this article, when searching [72] for the 'ideal' way to hold a dart. Ideal does not mean it works perfectly, well, or at all for you. If your present grip works, DO NOT alter it merely for change's sake. This article does discuss facts to consider with grip or release problems. Remember! No two players' grips are ever alike. NEVER change grips willy-nilly, despite how bizarre or unusual your present [◀72] one, without reason! Keep your mind open to new ideas. Any idea, no matter how small, could help.

Two ways to check for a correct grip are a static test and a

Jade Gardens   **Jim Kelly**

dynamic test. The test results should be identical, or close. When unlike, (rare) I suggest using the dynamic test's results.

Remember, any changes needed could seem extreme and, at first, awkward to put in practice. If a change feels clumsy, alter your grip slowly in small steps until achieved. Master grip changes in practice, never in a match! You alone can judge how fast to go. Never move ahead until at ease with a present step. Relax. Throw naturally, staying fully in control of darts.

First, the STATIC test: Shut your eyes. Curl your throwing hand into a loose fist. Then, open your hand slowly, spreading fingers and thumb widely. Open fully, until you feel tension in all fingers of your hand and palm. Let your hand become a loose fist while focusing elsewhere. Repeat with eyes closed and no care to your actions. Stop when some point on the thumb keeps touching an opposite spot. That spot could be on a finger, or palm. Note both points.

Second A DYNAMIC test to confirm these two points. Take your normal stance then throw 'air darts' at the board. Again, give NO thought to actions simply go through the motions. Imagine holding a pea and throwing it at a target. Avoid controlling your actions. Go through that motion ten or 12 times until sure that you are not guiding your actions.

Examine your thumb and finger's motion as you repeat your actions. Notice how the thumb and fingers snap open on a forward thrust, closing slowly coming back. Note how your brain controls opening and closing the thumb and finger(s). Your delivery motion is the brain's reflex act, pure and simple. You would need a great effort to erase these motions. Notice the way all actions repeat, despite how fast or slow.

Done right, you find the contact points in this second test the same ones found in test one. Keeping test results in mind, continue.

Balancing each dart on a finger, pinpoint its center of weight. Check that all three darts are alike. Sure of the two contact points, open your fingers just enough to slip in a dart. Repeat

Tamra Maus   **Russell F. Maus (RUSTY)**

48

until sure your two points are touching the dart. Checking often ensures placing these points exactly every time, neither too high nor low on the thumb. Verify both spots, not one alone. Confirm that the points remain opposite each other when holding the dart at or near its balance point. You could briefly put thin adhesive tape strips around darts to place the thumb or fingers.

First, find the spot on your thumb for the dart to rest. Place it well, considering the dart's angle.

Let all other fingers fall naturally in place, on or off the dart. Use fingers resting on the dart to steady it, aiding your delivery motion. Should a finger (or fingers) feel awkward, move the dart slowly back and forth for best fit. If moving the dart proves hard, its shape is probably wrong for your hand. You could move ill-fitting fingers, so one or more rest easily on the dart's surface. The catch is that fingers will return to their usual position when throwing. Avoid flicking a finger(s) placed on the dart's thumb side at release. Unwanted finger movement may alter the dart's flight, veering from a straight path. Anyone can throw darts. Few fully control themselves, their throw and dart.

Keep the thumb's contact point and test the opposing spot. If this fails, stay with the opposite point and move the thumb. The thumb provides power while fingers give control. Try to find an ideal balance.

Finding your correct grip is tricky. Some pros simply lay the dart across their fingers (at the proper angle) pin it with the thumb and fire. While this grip looks easy, know that much thought and effort went into it.

Any 'guide' finger(s) (those not aiding the thumb in throwing) should touch the dart lightly. We all have a different sense of touch. Test yours. Do not involve 'guide' finger(s) in throwing. Also, with too much thumb action try placing the dart against its side instead of the tip.

◀72 Test other dart configurations at a local dart store. A shop not letting you test, does not want your business. Should you see no other option, try a friend's darts. With a well-weighted set, that fits your hand shape, PLAY DARTS.

Jack McDonald   **Jim McDonald**

At release, your thumb and opposing point should be the last in touch with the dart. Otherwise, a dart may wobble. If they are not opposite, keep these two points at the same height or you may twist the dart.

With a stable dart move the thumb within its normal range of motion. This gives you several inches with which to work. To cure a wobbly dart, find the best spot for your thumb in that region. Place thumb and finger(s) where each exerts equal pressure giving the smoothest, straightest arc for your grip.

Throwing a dart correctly, your two contact points open after all other fingers move out of the way. Otherwise, a wobbly throw is likely, as forces applied to the dart remain uneven to cause problems. In straight-ahead throws, these two points open at once. Finger and thumb must open together when opposite each other. Throwing with points not opposing, the slower one exerts extra force on that side.

To grip, throw, and release a dart properly requires exact complex actions much too rapid for easy study. Simplify any motion by breaking each down into small steps. Then think clearly, what happens at each step? You may need to tip your dart up or down a bit to gain a correct arc. The ideal release is at the very top of your arms arc. Some darters cannot easily throw darts straight on without effort.

Do not monitor every motion of body, arm, hand and fingers while throwing. You <u>MUST</u> throw darts without thought other than focusing on the target. Other thinking simply makes efforts harder. With problems throwing your dart straight on, make adjustments. Adjust the thumb in tiny steps until darts fly smoothly.

Another point! Placing your thumb under instead of against the dart's side may make a big difference. With your thumb at its side, a dart begins dropping instantly. You gain two big pluses by resting the dart on your thumb. First, the dart rides on your thumb, supported for a much greater distance before release. Support lets you ease up on throwing, as you need not battle gravity as much. Second, this method gives more control of dart

John Sigel

and throw. If placing your thumb under the dart is awkward or impossible, try the squeeze method discussed in Article 55. The grooves formed give your dart support, but unlike the thumb. Squeezing makes repeating a grip easier.

PUSH OR PULL: A grip, forward of a dart's balance point pulls it to the board. Gripping at or behind this point is pushing the dart. Many pros think pushing is easier, more accurate and less tiring. Pushing the dart may also result in a greater upward arc. If unable to push, try a front-heavy dart. This may seem a petty point, but worth trying. No success! Forget the idea and return to pulling your dart.

To check tension, roll a dart slightly after setting your grip. A loose grip will slip and one too tight will not roll.

Hold darts in your non-throwing hand so you transfer and set the grip with no thought. Learn to know, by feel, when your grip is right. Never look at the dart, stay focused on the target.

Your grip is crucial and perfecting it very hard. Time spent working for answers, is valuable. You may find YOUR grip at once or sadly, like some, struggle for years with slow progress.

73   **GRIP VARIETY:** The easiest to master are four or five-finger grips. Most darters use one of those two. Players with stubby or extra-long fingers may find both useless. Most darters hold a dart with ease. The problem comes in placing darts into a stable arc toward the board. A darter should alter their grip for a proper release.

A three-finger grip, harder to use and control, raises a dart's front or pointed end. Players constantly landing low should test a three-finger grip. The extra work in mastering any grip warrants the effort, if you correct an awkward or faulty throw.

Keeping fingertips in touch with the dart is a sound rule. Break this rule if unable to go from four or five-fingers to three. Keeping your four or five-finger grip, simply move the dart. Lower the dart between thumb and index finger, below the fingertip. Move the dart as far down as the **◄73** index finger's second joint, or lower.

One finger contacting the dart at two points or along its length is like using a 3-finger grip. The advantages are one less controlling finger and an easier release. If needed, a third finger can help guide the dart.

When testing grips, avoid rushing to settle on a final spot. Minor changes may make for big gains while becoming familiar with a new grip. Positive changes aid control, helping scoring skills soar. A 'final' grip may be hard to reach in one step. This is true for all standard grips and variations.

Rarely used, a two-finger grip is hardest to use. Work on the two-finger grip if no other works. A top woman dartist uses a two-finger grip, doing notably well. Your grip must let you score well, while staying at ease.

Try holding your dart like a pencil. This grip is surely comfortable, relaxed and natural. Some experts warn against using this grip. Yet, do not abandon the method to quickly if results prove less than pleasing. Move fingers farther apart or closer together at many places on the dart. Include a dart's point in tests. I position my index finger and half my thumb on the dart's 2-inch point, placing the forefinger lightly on the dart body opposite the thumb. An unlikely grip using standard points.

Darts can react a great deal (for better or worse) to minor changes in finger placement. Should this process fail to help, at least you erased the pencil grip from possible use. Testing helps pinpoint flaws in grip or throw.

74 **CLOSE GROUPS:** Buy several rubber 'O' rings at a hardware store. Buy one of the 1, 2, 3 and 4-inch sizes (inside width). Dangle the rings from a finger to check each keeps its shape well.

Starting with the 4-inch ring, place it on the board using a common pin(s) or similar means. Move this ring around as you work to place all darts within its center. Once able to stay within the 4-inch ring, move down one size. If a full inch is too big a step, pick up rings in 1/2-inch steps. Then, the three and 1/2-inch size is next.

This process becomes much harder as the ring shrink. While a demanding system, do not be easily upset. If a step is too hard, return to the next larger ring until again confident. Work with the

Billy Lowe   *Donald Lemieux*

rings each practice, to group darts tightly. Even the best darters face problems staying within a 2-inch ring. The 1-inch size will test professionals.

Move the current test ring around regularly. Ideally, you should stay inside a ring no matter where it is hung. Avoid thinking like a darter I overheard saying; "I can put all my darts inside a 1/2-inch circle. My problem is getting the circle where I aim." Picture a ring around your target with each throw. Most darters find it easier staying within make-believe rings going for triples or bulls. Imaging is simple and yet powerful.

GUIDANCE: Guide, do not throw the dart as your arm and hand start forward. Released, missiles obey ┃ 75 ┃ flight's laws, not your wishes. Vital! Place darts in as near-perfect paths at release as possible.

Flights work to place darts into a straight line. An imperfect release applies more force on a dart's flight. The result is a dart going left, right, up, down or like a fish, some of each (fish tailing). You can see why such shots seldom score.

A well-thrown dart, like a spear, in theory should not need a flight to fly in a smooth, straight arc. In real life, this is untrue. No two throws are ever identical. Darts are also not (usually) front heavy and never as long as spears. Yet, for finding defects in your guidance system, throwing darts without flights may prove very useful.

Use a cheap set of darts with old shafts and NO flights. You need not dazzle anyone while finding grip or release flaws. Throw at an old board, if handy, because this test could damage or even ruin it. A great stand-in is an old sheet, blanket or rug. Fabrics absorb a dart's force leaving it little energy for bouncing back.

Although unneeded, you might draw a crude target on the fabric. Doing the test outside is wise, but not on a windy day! Indoors, test where darts cannot cause damage. Avoid any chance of injury. Keep people and pets out of the area. ALWAYS wear safety glasses!

Start around three feet from your 'board,' working back

Mark MacKenzie

toward the ochre. Throwing all darts normally, aim at a spot on the target. Throw easily, not hard! When testing, lock your eyes on the <u>DART</u> not the target. You care not where the dart hits, only how it gets there.

As you work back, watch where darts' first veer from a straight path. Any tipping action shows a lack of control. This first movement is hard to spot because dart throws takes a mere split second. Keep throwing and watch closely. In time you will see when and how it first tips.

When the dart hits, imagine it as a clock hand. Visualize the dart's tip at the center of the clock. What time is the dart's shaft pointing to on this imaginary clock? Of course, you want the dart not to tip at all. Rare players can do this feat seemingly at will. You need not become that expert, as dart flights are meant to fix minor errors.

Fixing flaws should prove easy when the shaft points up (12:00), down (6:00), left (9:00) or right (3:00) first. In each case, one small grip or throwing fault is possible. Yet, a shaft is more likely to point at some odd hour other than those four. This means you must find and fix two or more errors in your delivery.

The dart's first three to five feet, is the path's crucial area. Well-thrown darts rarely go off track beyond there. Fix that first three to five feet. Dart flights should then take care of the rest.

Working at correcting a throw, recall CORENA's rule, **CO**mfortable, **RE**laxed and **NA**tural. CORENA does not bar many variations, but excludes those you cannot handle. Use your effort's results as a guide. Awkward, yet positive, changes can rapidly become habits. Proper grips become a pure joy when you are able to hit any target like magic.

Despite millions of dart players, no two darters use a like mix of gear and methods. Yours is unique! Finding YOUR best dart, shaft, flight, ideal grip, throw and release are not easy. This search can be upsetting, seeming to take ◄75 forever. Yet, the rewards are worth any bother.

Erase your dart's side to side wiggles first then work on up and down movements. Throw in a straight line (viewed from above) from your eye or other starting point to the target. Else, the dart may fly sideways. Seen from the side, an in-flight line does travel in an arc.

Ideally, the line should run through a dart's center (end to end) at release. The wrist, elbow and shoulder should not stray from this imagined ideal line while throwing. To check, point your elbow at the target then drop it straight down. With a correct line, you need not move your hand's aiming point to either side.

If your ideal line fails any one of these tests, then to some extent you throw the dart sideways. The flight must now work to straighten the dart but it may strike the board before it does.

If able to hit your target with a wobbly dart, you will improve greatly by throwing straight. Checking your dart's straight-ahead placement (at release) should become part of your setup.

Erase your sideways problems, then focus on up and down wobbles. Throws may end with darts at the right angle. Nevertheless, watch your dart (in flight) to see how it gets there. You may see darts' wobbling up and down, sideways or both before impact. Darts may land perfectly, but wobbling kills accuracy on the way. Ask a player to watch your dart's arc from both the side and behind to spot movements.

Oddly, you may fix up or down errors by tilting a dart in the opposite way you would expect. For instance, the dart's rear may rise (toward 12 o'clock) then air grabs it, pushing its flight downward. Too much rising can result in a dart's rear ending below its front (toward 6:00). Logic says to alter your grip, so its rear is lower at the release point. Yet, lowering the flight end may raise it the same, or worse than before.

Try changing your grip so the back is now higher than originally. Contrary to common sense, holding a dart like this very often corrects its path. Flights now take hold at once, placing no other forces on the dart.

◄7

5

Keep working on your grip until throwing straight darts. Never be 100% content with your methods. Stay alert for physical body or arm changes.

Correct flaws until you throw straight darts. Then, adjust

your dart's arc with correct shafts and flights. The right combo helps with those small in-flight errors unfixed by throwing darts well. Focus on following through after every shot, keeping your dart pointed straight on (FORWARD). Your brain handles the rest.

YOUR INTERNAL GUIDANCE SYSTEM:
Your aiming point is not critical, but staying with the
same one is best. To prove that statement, try the next

| 76 |

test. Throw a dozen or so darts, at any target using your normal 'aiming' method. Then, move your arm a few inches higher (or lower); again throwing darts at the same target. Note how fast your brain adjusts, whatever change you make.

The secret here is positioning your arm where it is at ease. I strongly suggest keeping your hand as HIGH as possible with comfort. Why! The brain now works WITH gravity—much easier. You throw with less effort, as the elbow remains fixed. With a low starting point, your brain must adjust for throwing uphill. You must throw the dart harder while your brain controls any extra muscle needed to get it there. You may think this a small point, but any help for the brain is a big extra. The brain can then use its reserves on the important task of guiding a dart.

| 77 |

HAND SPEED: Are you familiar with the space program's lingo? If yes, you know the phrase 'window of time.' This term means, the ideal moment for placing a rocket into its planned orbit. Many factors need study such as weather and people.

Not reaching an exact altitude, speed and path at the right moment may burn fuel stored for later use in its mission. Wobbly crafts use more fuel. A fuel shortage would be tragic for a safe landing.

The arc of a dart is similar. You must put it into a
perfect arc (orbit) with minimum energy, releasing at
the right instant. Releasing a dart, at the wrong

| ◀77 |

'window' in your arms arc, will place it off track. No chance of hitting the target now exists. Consider. A throw takes about 1/8-second. You must release a dart within, at most, the time your hand travels around one inch. That 'window of time' for a scoring throw nears 1/100ths of a second.

How fast is the brain? A throw takes 1/8 or 12/100ths second. An eighth of a second is a short time. Yet, the trained brain easily controls 1/100th second spans.

Now 63, I never had fast reactions or any talent for judging time. Yet, with practice, I can freeze a stopwatch at 00/100ths six or seven times in ten, and three in a row. All the misses coming within 5/100ths second. Test yourself with a stopwatch. A few trial runs and you may do as well, most likely better. Never put down your brains ability or even newer players.

Your brain easily handles this brief 'window'. Still, problems start when hand speeds get too fast. Increasing hand speed shortens the 'window of time,' and makes placing darts in a proper arc harder. Simply common sense! Throwing faster will pass more energy to the dart. Extra energy makes a flight's job harder and the dart's wobbling worse.

You do need a certain minimum hand speed for the dart to reach its target. Yet, that speed is much slower than what most dart player's use. At first, slow your hand speed in practice to prove this fact. Your brain can now use that extra time for correcting other throwing problems. Slowing one's hand speed is hard as throwing fast is more normal. Reaching this goal, you will never regret trying.

THE HARDEST GAME. I consider CRICKET a | 78 | harder game than '01'. My record, playing CRICKET proves it true, for me anyhow. Other players think '01' games are worse because they must hit doubles. Better double scorers naturally win more '01' games.

Of course, this belief hurts my CRICKET game, missing many easy shots. Playing '01', I seldom throw at, and sometimes avoid some CRICKET wedges.

Winning at '01' is often a matter of making one final shot, with skill or luck. You may be the better shooter in a match, but pure luck may decide who wins. NO player (pros included) knows for sure where their next dart will land. Even with the skill to place three darts in the double bull is no guarantee. Putting three, four or more shots in a row beside a winning double's wire surely takes great skill. Losing by a wire width (or a bounceout) can test anyone's spirit. Do not let misfortune get you down, should you lose in this way.

To win CRICKET games you must score 21 hits on wedges and bulls. Yes, stray triples help greatly though you <u>rarely</u> win at CRICKET with lucky shots. At game's end, the bull area can look like a pinhead.

Tell the captain your strong and weak points. Let her decide when you play. Play games you dislike! I tried not playing CRICKET for a long time, until I HAD to play and then proved totally useless. I saw a stretch of over a year (17 games) without a win. Looking back, I lost about half those games by missing with ONE dart. The other half I judged lost no matter what my partner or I threw.

Seeing the singles value, trying harder with each shot became easier. Giving up after a few ugly throws is playing to lose, which I did! Never quit! That dart in hand often proves valuable later, to win. Strive to become a complete darter!

HEALTH: Your general health must stay excellent to throw the best darts at all stages of your darting career. Health problems will catch up with your dart game. You should improve slowly, but steadily, in steps. Throw daily, polishing all game facets. You should meet no trouble staying at your present skill level. Yet, an off game or match is entirely normal.

Despite your best efforts you may get worse slowly or swiftly when suffering health problems. Failing to pin down a reason, I urge you to see a doctor at once!

AUTHOR'S NOTE: This happened to me. An exam showed a life threatening disease. Having found this problem at an early stage, my doctor brought the ailment under control.

Some RX effects may seem faint while making you shaky throwing Darts. Sensing a problem, ask for medicine with fewer (or even free of) side effects.

HEIGHT: Extremes in stature could raise hurdles. A tall player sees as much trouble hitting Double 3 as a four-footer needing Double 20. Darters with height problems should stick with the basics. Bend at the waist to adjust.

Paul DiTullio | **VFW Post 9013**

Taller players ask for problems by lowering their arm instead of bending forward. Locking one's elbow is hard when dropping your upper arm. Check this action out in a mirror.

81 **IMPROVING:** Playing better Darts is a result of regular, correct practice AND league play. Practice an hour a day, every day, when possible. Repetition builds and fine-tunes hand-to-eye rhythm, poise, and harmony. Daily practice keeps the muscle tone of your dart arm and that vital 'mover' the brain, in shape. Your brain takes on all throwing details.

Better players never think about how to throw a dart. Smart dartists tell their brain where to throw then give up control. Skilled players give their brain TOTAL control. Experts throw so often the motion becomes second nature, like driving a car.

Daily practice may improve mechanics but still not make you a better dart player. League play alone, refines your dart game. Even doing well in practice, when first starting in a league, your mind is likely to go blank. You must then relearn the basics.

Do not worry about how you play, look and what others may think should you lose. Doing this, you try to seize control with your mind. It does not work. Giving your brain full control is critical.

Yielding control does not reduce your daily practice session's importance. It stresses practice's value!

INNOVATE: Remain forever alert to ways of **82** improving every part of your dart game. Growth is a simple series of small changes for the better. Polish your style and darts endlessly. Every dartist uses a special mix. No two darters own or use identical gear, stance, grip, throw, attitude or skill.

Find your best blend of skills and equipment. Constantly try new and novel ideas. Finding your dart's correct weight, shape, best shaft and flight style will take time. With a random approach, the quest may mean years. All players should test a variety of weights and shapes before buying better darts. Good dart shops allow testing.

Joe Muri

In practice, use anything to develop skills, even mechanical aids! Never use artificial means in matches, though. General use would soon outlaw them and spoil it for those players truly needing help.

JERKINESS: a lurching body or arm hurts accuracy, making a uniform dart delivery difficult. No, | 83 | hopeless! Sadly, many darters with this snag stay unaware of it. Those players knowing about this problem may not know how to fix it.

Awareness is the first, often biggest step! Ask others if you are guilty of movements (often unknown). If the answer is yes, tackle this problem! You cannot move ahead until clearing the big hurdle of an uncontrolled body. Often, merely knowing a problem exists is enough to tackle and beat it. The drills in this book help expose and beat all defects. See Article 112.

| 84 | **JITTERS OR NERVES:** Listed below are three ways to avoid or beat nervous problems. For best results, use at least two, but ideally all three.

1. Hypnotism or other means to relax.

2. Proper deep breathing.

3. Laughter.

1. Hypnotism works wonders at easing stress, yet those making less than ideal subjects, (receptive or not), may need many sessions. Low priced, handy hypnotists would cure many problems. Unlikely!

Your best option is using a cassette tape often, even daily. Strad Darts offers information about a 'Competition Preparation™' tape, recorded by a licensed hypnotist. | ◀84 | This tape can help all dart players.

2. Done right, deep breathing melts away tensions. You can learn that skill from this tape as well. Use the coupon at end of the book to inquire.

3. By far the cheapest and best remedy is laughter. Taking any game seriously is hard, even impossible, when laughing at one's faults. This is notably true when you find yourself getting too serious. Sadly, many find a light heart difficult. I make no

claims laughter is easy for anyone, but it is a truly potent tool!

With your physical game under control, consider using a self-hypnotic or meditation tape, just before matches. Use for calming nerves, or stifling fears and worries. Both relax and soothe your mind as you monitor and control your random thoughts.

Cold or sweaty hands (or feet) could indicate nervousness even if you are not feeling so. Getting jittery is normal and not shameful. Facing and coming to grip with facts is best. Ignoring tenseness is like sticking your head in sand. Others may not think you nervous, yet, you WILL find breathing hard! So, admit to nerves, and if nothing else laugh at your fears.

You may simply possess surplus nervous energy. Drain such energy by focusing on other darting problems. This might solve several issues.

Despite their skills, top-ranked US players tell me pros too get nervous before matches. A pro knows any dartist can get hot and win. I saw it happen. The big difference is pros can live with losing. From past matches money players know a negative sign is when they have no butterflies just before a game. An overconfident player is riding for a fall. Pros must redouble their efforts, every match. Dart masters do not fear losing yet work at keeping their mental edge. Mental health is a big reason these players are pros.

85 **KANGAROO:** Do not bounce around at the line. Changing your release point often confuses the brain. Controlling darts is hard enough throwing from one spot. Always launching a dart from the same spot in space will ease the brains work.

Avoid moving the body in any way. Swaying left or right will cancel a perfect dart. If you MUST move when throwing, go toward the board. Yet, even forward tipping should be slight for best dart control. The only motion needed is from elbow to fingers. No other movements help!

Dipping (bending at the knees), tiptoeing and falling forward are all big no-nos. Some darters do all those on each throw

Ralph Walker

(looking like they have a hot foot) and still play decently. Imagine the improvement if riveted to one spot and moving only the forearm and hand! The only bouncing needed is back from defeats.

86 **KILLER INSTINCT:** You need not win any dart game quickly, but avoid fooling around in a match. Simply go ahead and finish the game. Do not torment rivals like a cat toying with a mouse. They may bite.

I see excellent darters lose by making light of others' skills, or puffing theirs up, after easy games. Hard work alone wins dart matches not a big head! Think back. How often do you play great back to back legs? For me the next one is often a struggle. Like taking one's press readings to heart, you believe losing cannot happen. Thinking it true, you stop watching the finer points and go rapidly downhill.

A teammate threw a 10-dart first game of 301 against a young woman new to Darts. She looked totally lost, failing even to get in during that game. The second of the best two of three legs started the same way. He seemed able to score at will and was soon looking at his pet winning double. The poor woman was still not in and now flustered almost to the point of tears.

Instead of simply finishing the game, he did something I had never seen. He started to throw off- handed for his double, with no luck. She became a tiger, getting in and out in record time. The final leg proved a farce. He was now the one struggling to get in while she blew him away—to cheers from BOTH teams. Remember! Kittens have claws they can use.

KISS: Keep It Short and Simple! No other advice is more fitting. Make your delivery, and all other game **87** facets, simple and as exact as possible. Simplicity improves Darts, like no other talent.

LOOSEN UP: Do you forever shoot low or sense that you steer instead of guiding the darts? One reason **88** could be excess wrist tension from mentally steering the darts. For a smooth, natural release, free up your wrist. A possible cure is wiggling the wrist freely when shooting. Doing

Rich Mongeau   **Joan Brannagan**

this right, you look as if pumping your arm before throwing.

One way to loosen up is to hold the forearm vertical and simply let your wrist fall limply forward. Then, pull your wrist back (with the forearm), letting it swing freely like a limp dishrag. Not using any wrist muscles during this motion is vital. Some may find their darts scatter while perfecting this strange motion.

Notice how with your wrist loose darts fly faster and smoother and with little effort! The dart's arc is flatter too. You can now throw slower and focus on your accuracy. However, many darters find pumping an awkward motion, no matter how often they try.

Once able to keep a loose wrist, drop the first motion from your delivery. Start with hand hanging freely, going on from there. This forward hand pump forces your wrist to remain free. Once your mind accepts a limp wrist, stop pumping, if you wish.

Check the elbow once your wrist pivots freely. Use a minimum of muscle to work the elbow joint. Master both the wrist AND elbow's free motion. Lack of muscle tension makes it easier to throw each dart with equal energy. A smooth uniform force greatly reduces soaring or dipping darts. Of course, this free motion must not alter your elbow height from the floor. Looseness may hurt if you are unable to lock your elbow height firmly, with shoulder muscles. Darts could become more erratic. You cannot know until trying this method.

LOSING: You can never become a WINNER in Darts (or any other sport) until accepting losing— with true grace. First, work on outward calmness, then strive to face losses inside. Losing gracefully is basic and surely, the hardest lesson for each dart player. Learn to lose! Doing so, will boost your delight and spur the desire to improve faster than other methods.

89

Fantasy is expecting to win every time you play no matter how expert you become. This attitude badly affects every dart. That idea could lead to your game's ruin. Forget losses. Simply

| *Moe Dellolio* | *Diana Tucker* |

refuse to remember! Play with an attitude of "I don't give a damn whether I win or lose, but I'm going to enjoy myself!" You will still lose some games thought won and win others deemed lost. Those games will balance out though. Adopt a cheerful air. You will enjoy Darts more, while improving.

MIND OVER MATTER! Losing does not MATTER if you do not MIND. Players who think or state, "I cannot lose" are losers in peers' minds. DO NOT become obsessed with winning.

Striving for perfection at Darts applies useless pressure every time you pick up a dart. You can never enjoy the game to its utmost. Think! With no risk of losing, you would quickly become bored with Darts. You need not enjoy losing, NO ONE DOES or ever will or should! Face the facts! You can and WILL lose! Do so with polish. Darts then becomes a winning sport for all players. Be a winner, not a whiner.

Give every match your best efforts, but never live or die on ANY game's outcome, despite how big it seems. No connection exists between a match's result and your self-worth. A 'MUST WIN' outlook, is a loser's view. Remember, on any given night half the players lose. LEAGUE PLAY IS A TEAM SPORT: Better to lose three points and have your team win 8-3 than take three, losing the match 3-8.

Winning may make you more popular, with fellow players anyway. Winning can never make you a better person. Losing should not make you less liked or mean failure. Mates cannot ask you to give more than your best. Should a team expect more, find another.

◄89 Nursing a bruised ego conflicts with your ability to win future games. Avoiding being hurt, we often repeat our errors. If that empty feeling, after losing, gnaws for over a few minutes or bothers your sleep you have not learned how to lose!

Darts is a game. Games mean fun. Many players take Darts too serious, acting as if at a wake! Laugh when a game goes wrong. Laughter with a broad smile works wonders for you, your game and partners. Enjoy dart matches whether winning or

Bob Parlante

losing. You limit joy and training finding pleasure only in winning.

A joyful outlook can relax you more than any other tactic known, while keeping your mind on the game. By laughing at follies, you will stay cool, thus calming nerves and game. Live by the winning darter's motto: "EXPECT THE BEST, ACCEPT THE REST."

Many runner-ups play Darts – but never 'losers'. No one who truly loves this game could ever deserve a loser's title. Anyone who plays Darts properly is none other than a WINNER.

Someone coming in at matches' end should have to ask, "Who won?" They should see only smiles and handshakes whether a team wins or loses.

Mirror those dart players to whom you do not mind losing. Remember how you feel when winning, show empathy for a winner when losing. Look at Darts not as playing against, but WITH others.

Play Darts to win or for pleasure. Oddly, either attitude can lead to the other. Only one team can win, not necessarily the best or most talented. A game won by a sliver of steel landing on the right side of a wire involves luck. The more evenly matched players are the truer this becomes. Make Darts fun BEFORE expecting to win, not AFTER.

In an eight-team division of nine players per team (72 total), only nine can be (official) winners. The best player's team may finish last. The top team can carry the least talented player(s). Like Life, Darts is rarely FAIR. All players with good attitudes are 'winners'.

LUCK OF THE DRAWS: Many fine darters do not enter these contests. Asked why, many confess feeling they lack the skill or are afraid of looking foolish. Their fear is normal. Yet, it cannot stand up to facts! Most shooters are surely capable enough. Dartists, like everyone, fear unknowns! After a few matches, 'luck of the draw' is like any other game. Breaking the ice is hard.

Luck of the draws and tourney players, are no different from

90

Mark O'Connor (BUBBA)

other darters. Veterans know how hard breaking in is, from experience, and show great empathy for new entrants. Most darters are truly great people. No one will yell or put you down if playing poorly. Drawing newcomers is a risk and the reason darters call this game <u>LUCK</u> of the draw. Old hands at draw games accept playing with new darters; realizing staying in the running is tough. The opposite can happen too. Paired with a better shooter, they may play great darts.

Playing in local, state, regional and finally national tourneys is a great way to improve your dart game. You play high-caliber shooters every game. No better way exists for advancing so quickly. At ease in these settings, league play becomes a snap.

Try 'luck of the draw' matches. The worst result is you might not enjoy these bouts. You may also be taking a first step toward national ranking prestige. Where else can world-class darters begin their climb? All top-ranked darters took this route. Win your share of games, once truly believing you belong.

MEDIA: Darters should stay up on all dart world news. Can you name current top shooters, male and | **91**

female? Knowing is not crucial. Yet, if unable, you cannot be reading any dart publications.

Darts is a fast changing sport. New ideas and items come out every month. How else can you stay current on where to buy new products, future events, match results, or the pros' hints?

Keep current, with the dart media. One great idea could help your game immensely. You will find books, magazines, audio & video instruction tapes by pros and other aids at good dart stores. Watch magazine ads. You will see many items of interest.

MENTAL BLOCKS: Dart players often build hurdles with false beliefs. For instance, many think | **92**

scoring on the 20 wedge is important because just about everyone else does. I know of no catch or shame in scoring on other numbers. Winning steadily, on an odd wedge, any groans heard are your rivals. The sole benefit in throwing 20's is if you are trying for a perfect game in 501 (nine darts). You need extra darts playing another wedge. In 301, finishing in six darts is also possible playing other high wedges.

Sure, throwing 60 or a ton (100) can look and feel great, but a few misses reduce your points per dart average fast. Are you unsure about easily hitting other high number(s)? Occasionally, spend a practice session throwing 50 or 100 darts at each wedge 14 through 20 plus the bull area. Your number, is where you score best!

Include the 14 wedge. Fourteen is the highest scoring wedge with an upright (vertical) triple. Fourteen and the wedges on each side of it total 34. Other three wedge groups total more. They own horizontal (flat) triples though. A miss on one of those wedges can result in a low score. Missing 14 often yields nine, sometimes, 27 or 33. Great results are notably true when your darts stay in an upright line. Off their game, many excellent dartists take (brief) refuge on the 14 wedge. Add this option to your arsenal.

Another fallacy held by some 301 players is they must go in on Double 20 or other high numbers. Most big doubles present a tiny 'upright' (5/16-inch) target. Many players find staying in a vertical line much easier and safer than flat. Until easily hitting 'flat' doubles, go in at the board's sides. Test the Double 6 and 11.

Once a match is over, who cares that you got in (after many tries) on Double 20. Painfully true when your rival wins while you are above 200. Little chance exists of getting in when missing 'flat' doubles. Misses at 'upright' doubles may land in six or eight others. The first double has the edge, not the biggest—Double 1 included.

◄92   Some shooters hurt their game when needing bulls, 'thinking' the bullseye a hard shot. The total bull area is about twice an outer double. Three times a triple. NEVER fear the bull area and not score there.

Proving this inability a mental block, try this: Ask a shooter who admits fearing the bull (Bullitis) to throw 50 shots at the 6 wedge's large single area. Repeat this exercise on the 11 wedge. Also try it yourself.

Jim Depatie

Tally total hits in both areas. Doubles or triples are misses. Then, using a #2 pencil, trace a 7/16-inch flat washer's edges in the center of both wedges. This creates two rings looking exactly like the bull area. Ask the shooter to throw 50 darts at those two areas again. The one change is an added 'bullseye' drawn in each wedge.

Compare the second tests results with the first. The second scores are usually lower. Many shooters become uneasy simply seeing a 'bullseye'. Darters who 'can't' hit certain numbers suffer this trait.

Should some problem (physical or mental) prevent you from hitting any target, MOVE! Normally a no-no, on occasion, moving may prove a positive step.

Doubling in, or out, in '01' games, does not mean you must use certain doubles. Trying for doubles that you hit only every 9 or 12 shots makes little sense. Instead, go for a double you can make in three shots.

Knowing you can hit any double, including double bull, go for it, at once. Waiting merely gives the mind a chance to raise doubts. Go for an out shot any time an opponent(s) can possibly win their next throw. This accents the value of hitting all doubles in practice.

CRICKET demands sound strategy to win regularly. Any two games of CRICKET are rarely alike. Times arise when you must throw at a number other than the next lower one. For instance, you cannot score on closed wedges. Going for numbers out of order may also confuse opponent(s), giving you an edge. Psyching out is much more common in CRICKET than '01' games.

◄92

Avoid this CRICKET trap, which comes up often.

Needing one bull to win, you miss with your first dart. You note your rival(s) still needs one 15 and two bulls. In case of a miss at the game shot with the final dart you throw your second dart at and hit a 15. This is to make the other team hit an added bull. With that notion, you miss the bull. Imagine your woe when they pick up a 15 and win with two bulls—not three! The single 15

Mattie Perno   **Bill Lee**

68

added too few points to force another bull. Your best play. Throw all three darts at the bull. Always go for the win!

The point is; DO NOT play any Dart game without thinking. Throw every dart with a purpose.

93 | **MIND CONTROL:** Learn to put your mind into cruise control. Tell your brain what you need then turn over control. The more you crave it the harder winning is. Your mind cannot resist taking control if results rule. (I throw great darts when sick and not thinking about winning). The Eastern art of 'no mind' may sound easy; placing thoughts in idle is hard. You need not slip into a daze, trance or stupor. Simple stay detached to each throw's results. Let your mind remain a spectator to the brain's handiwork. Your ticket is many hours of practice. Tell your brain "I'll watch, dazzle me!"

Your opponent is nervous, maybe more so than you. Awareness here provides a big edge. Follow through by appearing calm and confident in play. Always assume success. Think, I intend to win and believe it.

Learn to relax by throwing at a totally blank target with no spider (wire). Draw a circle, 13½-inches wide, on a board or other material that darts can stick into and stay. Aim for keeping all darts within the marked area. Easy! Yes! Notice how relaxed and sure you feel. Now, with a regular board, try hitting two double bulls in a row. Hard! VERY! Notice how tense and uncertain you got. I wonder why the big difference. Well, the second aim is a wee bit harder. You would play better with your mind and body in the first state I am sure.

Learn to grip and throw a dart correctly at the right target. Turn the rest over to your brain. ◄93

Alpha is a mental state, midway between wide-awake and normal sleep. At the line, put your mind into an Alpha state—daydream! Stand-up meditation results.

Never link effort with the outcome! Give your best during every game despite the results. At times, giving 100 percent, you gain nothing. A thought then arises "what's the use" and you think of quitting. You must see how difficult the sport of Darts is.

Dennis Seeley

Always winning easily, no challenge exists.

Other times you will win with little effort, thinking "Yes, the way to go!" With little difficulty you stop trying, soon losing the drive that kept skills sharp—never mind improving! Lack of effort catches up with you. Thinking you can go on winning, without trying, one day WILL ruin your game, plunging you into despair. A comeback can then be long and hard.

94 **A MIRROR:** Use a full-length mirror at your practice board for watching form. Buy cheaper mirrors in big outlet stores. A 12X48-inch wood frame is ideal.

Place this mirror on the floor or hang it using two 'L' hooks and eyes. Pivot the mirror to view your entire body. While standing on one leg, if unable to throw decent darts easily, you likely lunge, dip or go up on toes. Now, with the mirror, you cannot avoid seeing flaws or jerky movements. Form may appear perfect, but defects creep in when least expected. Use a mirror to catch faults before they become habits.

95 **MUSCLE MEMORY:** Train your arm to throw smoothly and true without thought. The brain does control every motion made, but repeated use makes it pure reflex. Once delivering dart after dart accurately, without thinking, you have _**IT**_. You gain muscle memory only by constant practice. Once in a groove, a few warmup throws will bring peak performance.

MUSCLE TONE: The better your arm's shape is to begin with, the faster it rebounds from short-term **96** abuse. Practice every day to improve. Missing a day occasionally cannot set you back a great deal. Your love for Darts decides practice habits.

Avoid physical excess before dart matches. Hard manual work, or periods of dart arm disuse, can hurt. The chief reason pros practice hours daily is to stay fit. Pros work to build their muscle's tone, memory and reflexes to peaks then work to stay at those levels.

Nonuse is the *main reason darters improve so slowly,* if at all. Once throwing well, you need a measure of 'hands-on' use to

Jim Milioto   **John VanVoorhis**

stay sharp.

ODD SINGLE NUMBERS: The ability to hit | 97 |
triples when needed, is a first-rate player's mark.
Making odd single wedges with one shot is a great player's talent. Hitting a one, three or five to arrive at an out shot can seem like shooting for a double bull. You find this painfully true when facing an odd total of 17 or less. You usually bust when missing low odd wedges. With 19, should you aim for 3 hitting a single 17 you need D-1. Most would prefer another Double.

Taking three or four throws to hit an odd single wedge, big leads can dry up fast. Becoming upset, you will rarely make an out shot after finally hitting that odd number.

Hitting odd single wedges, when needed, is a vital skill. At least once each practice hit the 1, 3, 5, 7 and 9, in whatever order, with the fewest tries. Hit each wedge in no more than three, ideally one shot.

| 98 | **OBSERVE:** Watch fine darter's methods at every chance. Try any new tactics seen, in practice. Notice especially how little better players move. Their throws always look silky smooth and effortless too.

Great darters refine their stroke to basics, remaining in control of the dart. Notice how better players stay calm and cool, win or lose. Copy their poise. Coolness under fire helps your game immensely.

| 99 | **OCHRE or TOELINE:** The ochre is there for a reason. Obey the line! NEVER go over a toeline, when playing—period,. Should you ignore warnings, do not express shock when a protest voids a great score. Going over the line is cheating. Ignore this rule and risk someday finding no one with whom to play.

| 100 | **THROWING WITH YOUR OFF-HAND:** Start each practice session by throwing with your off-hand. The hand you use to hold your darts. Finding this motion awkward at first, hang in there. Begin slowly, throwing a few darts. Build until delivering pain-free.

Start by throwing until keeping most darts within the triple

Brendan Harrington

ring. NOW, begin the following cycle. First, hit all singles, then doubles, finally triples and bulls. Stick with the goals until scoring on every target.

The off-hand program takes time. Do not rush or give up quickly. Finishing your first complete cycle, drop all singles on all further cycles. With each shot, throw as you do with your playing hand.

This idea is not as foolish as some may think, and for various reasons. Someday you may need to swap hands because of an accident or disability. Darters often use the off-hand method to decide partners in team games. Give this plan a chance. Results may delight you.

This program is a great mental booster, as seen the first time hitting back-to-back doubles or triples. It will improve your focusing abilities too. How! Your brains left side controls the right hand while its right side manages the left hand. You will use your whole brain during workouts now!

This routine expands the brain's intuition and imaging centers, two vital skills for better darts. You might learn a few tricks for your regular hand. This routine shows what darters with such eye problems endure.

To prove the off-hand delivery's usefulness, I will show what this tactic did for me. After one month of throwing 21 darts daily, left-handed, I kept most of my darts within the triple ring.

I then started my first cycle. Throwing awkwardly, this took me 30 days. The second cycle (no singles) took ten days, the third only eight.

Throwing normally, the total shots previously needed to double around, (double bull too) dropped ◀**100** notably. I went from 100—120 to 60—80! My dart's per double average fell from 5 1/2 to 3 1/2. A huge drop, in only three months, after two years of very little progress.

101 **YOUR OPPONENT:** The dartboard is your foe! Whatever dart game you play, winning always comes down to you against the board.

CRICKET may appear more a match of wills than skill. Yet,

Tom Matson   **Jim Welsh**

getting down to basics, a player must hit her targets to achieve tactics. Never become upset when sensing a rival is trying to embarrass you. Not being a mind reader you cannot know his thoughts. Rarely is there only one winning line. A player's aim is to win.

If scoring at every chance in CRICKET seems your foe's flair, they may be making up for a weakness on bulls. Coming back with bulls (your strong point); you are only defending a game position, not for revenge.

Thinking another darter is trying to degrade you (true or not) gives away the upper hand. You now count two strikes. First, you gave up the mental edge. Then, trying for revenge, your target shrinks. Missing here could really anger you. Anger destroys your game and very soul. Confused, the brain works erratically.

Are you now down for the count? Probably! Anger is a great evener, making the worlds best beatable. Simply play the board wisely, weigh all options and go on throwing your best darts.

PARTNERS: Never gripe when paired with a weak player(s). Should this partner(s) overhear, you can usually write off that game. Work instead to build their confidence. Results could please.

102

A player does not need it pointed out when failing to carry his fair share. He knows! Use this occasion to show (with tact) weaker or new players how to improve. Beginners advance at various rates. Think. We all started somewhere. Natural darters are rare.

Most new darters wanting to become regular, valued players gladly listen to hints. Newcomers taking Darts seriously will improve. You may one day want them as a partner. Always support and cheer a partner(s). If a partner is doing well, you may catch her spark. When not, your support may turn her game around.

Never blame a partner for losing. If he did, they know very well, caring little for your sarcasm. Stay positive. Say, "next time", "bad luck" or "great try."

Build harmony with whomever you play, rivals included.

Tom Coolidge

You never know when rivals may become teammates—this happens to me often.

PATTERNS: Know your normal game patterns. Be ready to adjust quickly should changes occur **103** without warning. How do you feel before and during matches—tight and nervous, or relaxed and assured? Do you know when you throw enough warmup and are truly ready? Are you a slow starter, finishing strongly, or vice versa?

How do you react when tired or pushed to play well? Are you a leadoff shooter or better as an anchor? Do you give up easily or a bulldog who never quits?

You must know these answers and many others, to play to your full ability. Concerning your traits, avoid remaining unaware. Know your strengths AND faults. Insight builds game mastery, helping you exert self-control. You also know where you need to improve.

104 **PLATEAUS:** Like other skills, Darts becomes harder to improve on as one gets better. At first, new dart players make rapid gains every day. Beginners stay more open to advice, eagerly trying new methods. Sadly, later, their fire may cool. A closed mind is no asset, especially in Darts.

We all find getting beyond given skill levels difficult in any sport. Many dartists reach some stage then (who knows why) simply stop trying to improve. That is the ideal time for a darter to stay open to ideas, trying minor style changes.

Even without faults, steps up do get smaller, coming further apart. NOW Darts becomes a mind game. Keep looking to get better, at high levels that involves lots of PRACTICE!

NEW PLAYERS: I can take losing, (to better darts) but like many, hate forfeits. Losing several **105** weekly matches in a row because of no-shows can dismay any team. Inform your captain promptly when you are unable to play.

If you simply wish not to compete, for reasons or not, talk it over before quitting. The captain cannot read your mind. The chemistry simply may not brew (for you) with that group. Discuss problems, small or large, openly. You may think your

Diane Szymczak   *Tom Barry*

gripe obvious, but she may be totally unaware. At worst, she will respect your honesty, even if unable to agree on a cure.

Should you decide to quit, do so with tact. Avoid attacks on mates even when (you feel) them earned. Once word gets around of your ATTITUDE, finding a team willing to use you will prove hard. You may think you are through 'forever.' Drop out calmly. Time changes outlooks and values. Someday you may want to play again. Avoid rashly burning your bridges.

New darters are often eager, planning to become pros overnight. Beginners are the hardest to rely on too. New players become lax about showing up for matches if their team is not at or near first place after a few short weeks. Sharing a losing cause is torture for newcomers with little team loyalty or love for Darts. Winning is not everything and can often be the worst way to begin a darting career. Also, get word to the team somehow if you will be tardy. Showing up late, you cannot expect to play unless the captain knows.

Learners must be aware that building a winning squad takes time, often years. On teams with talented darters, rookies would get little playing time, seeing use simply as a reserve. With a building team, she plays regularly, a break few amateurs see.

| 106 | **PLAYING TIME:** "Why must I practice," you may ask? "I play in two leagues each week now!" Mainly, the problem is time. You must throw enough darts daily to stay at your present skill level—use it, or lose it! This does not even consider improving talents.

Figure how long you really play in matches? Three hours is a long match. Six players on each team equals 12 darters total. Playing in every game, (CRICKET, Team '01' and Singles, a darter averages 15 MINUTES. Ten minutes each is more realistic, wasting some five minutes, warming up, and fetching darts and other non-playing periods. *TEN MINUTES!* Playing three nights a week (a lot for many darters) this totals a mere one-half hour a week.

Consider this; to stay sharp, some pros throw upward of eight hours or more, <u>every day!</u> See why you do not improve as

Herbert Blanchard (BUD MAN)

wished?

You must know how long to throw before a match to play at peak form. Get needed time on practice boards, if open, shortly before games. Throwing more each day should shorten your warmup periods.

EXTRA LONG POINTS: Touring dart players have used these longer points for years. The 1¾ and 2-inch points are becoming popular with more dart players. You must decide if long points might help. | 107 |

Fixed steel-tipped darts normally come with 1½-inch points (before inserted). The same is true of moveable steel-tipped darts. Note! You can buy darts with points up to two inches long. Replace existing dart tips with these longer points also, if you wish.

Benefits claimed for longer points: A more visible target as the dart body ends farther from the board's surface. Extremely tight groupings are possible as three points can actually fit in one hole.

POISE: At the line, display a calm poise and a polite manner. If nervous, a confident air rests a bit | 108 | easier each time you play. Poise under fire becomes habit. Acting like a winner, you are half way there. Shake hands with rival(s) before <u>and</u> after matches.

Stay a gracious loser, more so, a humble winner. Never gloat or brag in or after a match. Cocky players ask for big letdowns when failing to play up to potential. Avoid giving a rival an added reason for beating you. Let your darts do the talking.

POSITION: Placement of ones' feet and the body's angle to the line is your position. No one way is | 109 | 'correct.' Every darter's position is unique. Keep testing until finding _**your**_ spot.

Find a spot where you easily throw relaxed and natural darts and stay there. You can always change later. Assure any switch is not a step backward.

Altering position, you might need to change stance, grip, delivery or all three. The brain figures your position in all its

| *Laura Shepherd* | | *Bob Shepherd* |

plans. Sudden changes can overload it, making quick adjustments hard. Fine-tuning, expect periods of poor darts. Test new positions—in practice.

Possible spots for your feet include, but are not limited to. Both feet straight-ahead, one foot's side against the ochre or any other angle in between. Do not go over the ochre. However, nothing says feet must touch the toeline. If you score better from (ANY distance) behind the line, do so. Keep feet close enough so shoes touch or far apart, whatever is comfortable. Wider is more stable, but may prove awkward. Best form keeps feet flat on the floor. However, I do see pros with a rear foot on tiptoe.

Vital! Place feet, so your arm is in line with the board's center. From here, any double adds a mere 1/4-inch to the dart's path. Standing, facing the board's side adds more than 1 1/8-inches to the dart's flight to doubles on the board's opposite side. Your darts can drop a great deal in this extra time and distance.

110 **POSITIVE:** How did you react to your first 180, round of nine or three double bulls? Wonder, shock, then sheer joy are the normal emotions, you may think "I've thrown three perfect darts, I don't need to prove any more" even feeling tempted to quit.

Most players realize, "Hey, I did that once, I can do it again." Belief in skills is the root to ones positive mental outlook. This attitude, is THE KEY to all future growth of one's darting skills. Nursing this, "I can," seed you grow with every perfect shot. Turn "Can I?" to "I can!"

The result is a growing sense of confidence, a quality every great darter must enjoy. Ignore all missed shots and lost games. Think positively. With the proper attitude, all shots are possible.

PROPER PRACTICE: A vital subject for all dart players working to improve their game is PROPER **111** PRACTICE. Sadly, a topic agreed on by few. The important point is building a positive mental attitude MORE than the manual skill of hitting certain targets. Regard practices in this way: finding YOUR stance, grip and throw hit each target at least once. The brain now knows all it needs to know.

Steve Koss
Billy Rocheleau

Never worry about results when practicing. (However, see article #134). Develop methods during practice. Hone skills here and results will follow. Darts, like all else in life, returns what you invest. Expecting to throw great darts using untested methods is like asking a pianist to perform with boxing gloves.

Learn to throw darts uniformly every time, turning control over to your brain. This seems a simple way to deal with a precise skill, but true.

A VITAL POINT! PRACTICE WITH OTHERS ANY TIME YOU POSSIBLY CAN.

Average dartists differ little; maybe 5% in their actual skill levels, from great ones. The other 95% dwells in their mind set. Candid money dart players readily admit this to be true.

Natural born dartists can do it all, without training or mental effort. Unless equally gifted, (few are) you may spend years finding YOUR stance, grip and delivery. Test each skill this book probes.

Your job is finding what works for you. Keep in mind, no darter throws darts exactly like anyone else. No player throws two darts alike either. Your goal is making all shots as alike as possible.

112 **PRACTICE AID:** Your physical goals: Stand without moving, throwing straight, true, darts with minimum arm motion. You need all these physical skills to play winning Darts.

PRESENTING THE PRO DART
(PRACTICE) PLATFORM™
Your Personal Dart Tutor. Simple, POTENT! ◄112

You may best gain your darting goals by using The Pro Dart (Practice) Platform™. Flaws in stance or throw, cause platform movement resulting in missed shots. Mastering its first setting, move outer bumper sets closer to the three permanent center ones. Each new setting makes steadying the platform a bit harder. Focused efforts force users to refine methods to gain lasting control of all their movements.

DIRECTIONS FOR USING

Mel Laughton   *John Carrier*

Use on a solid surface. With its bumper side down lay the platform behind the toeline. Step onto the platform's center, staying behind line 'A'. Your brain will adapt quickly to the added height. Position the rear foot first, then the front one, under your throwing arm. Start by setting your front foot's edge at line 'A'. Choosing a stance, move the platform so your body angle with toeline and board is right. The platform may extend over the toeline, not your feet!

Dismount by stepping off with your front foot first. Get on and off correctly, every time! If your feet cannot fit onto the platform, consider a new stance. Extreme stances rarely prove stable enough to throw consistent darts.

Gently rock the platform in all directions. Become aware of its motions, and your reactions. If you lose your balance, simply step off or let the platform settle on an edge. Once at ease, practice normally.

The platform alerts you at once to faults, such as swaying, rocking, tiptoeing, lunging or other flaws. Then, work at getting rid of any faults you find. Try moving feet or shifting the weight on your legs. Standing motionless and reducing throwing motions helps greatly. Explore all options, adopting any resulting in less activity. No set answers exist to all problems. The platform gives added awareness, providing a means for erasing most of them.

Conquering the first step, inch slowly to the platform's front edge to amplify remaining problems. Reaching the edge, stay there! NEVER GO BEYOND! Then, work through the other bumper steps. Check each bumper set is identical after every move. Be patient and go slowly. Gain control of each step before moving on to the next. Mastering the final step, you merit a hearty "well done." Rewards are a rock-solid stance, and a better game. Daily platform use stops a return to old habits or starting new ones.

Built and used, as directed, The Pro Dart (Practice) Platform™ will work as claimed. See BOOK BONUSES for how-to-build it plans.

113 **PRIORITY ONE:** Throw each dart at the correct target, to your best ability. You cannot alter past darts.

Becoming upset over missed throws is futile. Avoid excuses, accept facts, and then go ahead. Getting upset can only hurt your dart game.

Concern for future darts produces like results. Better dart players always plan their next shot. Looking ahead is great strategy. Yet, when the moment comes to throw, clear your mind. Tell your brain what to hit. Stay in the present. Do not meddle. Use your brain.

PSYCHING OUT: Using a rival's mind for gaining an edge. In many ways, all dart players use mental ploys to varying degrees. Meek players try to get tough ones to let up 'a little bit.' Braggarts try to talk their way into winning. Everyone uses mental tricks, although we may not notice.

114

Openly used, psyching is an unfair, brazen form of cheating. A game should decide the better dartist, not the best heckler. Taunts cheapen the game and its players. Avoid anyone using this practice. Tell rude players their act is uncalled for and not in Dart's spirit.

Realize psyching out is simply human nature, done by all. Seeing this fact, no player can get the mental edge without your okay. Stay alert!

PUSH THROW: If throwing a dart in the usual way feels clumsy, try the push shot. You may think pushing a dart requires little change in delivery—not true. Your motion does change! Pushing results in letting the dart go at a new point, with your arm in a greater upward sweep. These changes may not help, but worth trying facing problems. "Shooting from the hip" is a great method for instinct shooters.

115

The pushing method's pluses! First, you may feel an added sense of control from using new muscle sets. Second, pushing might fix the problem of forever landing below your target because the dart arcs less. This throw is closest to a single overall arc. Pushing extends your arm a few inches farther. Your mind focuses on delivery, while the brain guides the rest.

A pushing motion is much like a wrist shot, a hard way to

Robert Graham (DUTCH)

throw darts. Throwing differs in the elbow action. Pushing a dart, you must let your elbow float. Normally a no-no! Like a wrist shot, you guide the dart (with your wrist) not simply going with the flow. This motion is hard enough with a rigid elbow, more so when loose.

Some darters, most often women, push instead of throwing their darts. Small wonder, playing Darts is a task for some. Pushing darts is okay, but harder and more tiring than throwing them.

These comments should not stop you from trying the push shot. For some darters, this motion is an easier, more natural one. Should this method prove hard to tame, you then value the catapult shot's ease. Keep adapting to improve your game!

116 **QUARRELS:** Never raise your voice or become upset to the point of possible violence. No dart match should ever get that serious. Doing this will throw any player off their game. Settle problems calmly. Before a fight results.

I saw two near fights in ten years of playing, but know of no case of darters coming to actual blows. Considering the pub setting, I think this amazing. In each incident, someone (not a player) wanted to get into the act after a few too many. We quickly tamed both and the matches ended without problems.

A few dart players let themselves become upset and start shouting. No need exists for this to occur. When anything gets under your skin, speak to the captain; let him handle it (see Article 150). Letting anger rule, your game goes out the window. DO NOT LET IT!

QUIRKS: We all display peculiar little quirks. Watch for oddities in others as you may see something **117** usable. Most are negatives, though. Avoid picking up every poor habit you see.

RECORDS: Keep your high points always visible. I mount my practice board on a 48-inch **118** plywood square. Throwing great darts, I make a dated record on my board with an ink marker. I Then look at all recorded high spots when down on my game.

When you hit 180 or other three triples, record it! Ditto, for three double bulls, '01' or CRICKET games finished in less than

X darts. Record all big ins, outs, double or triple strings of more than 3-4-5, whatever.

True, those events are rare at first. All the more reason to keep a record, so the mind grasps the brain's power (the ultimate darter). Throw better alone and then in league play, as records are always visible.

119 **REPOINTING:** This is a cheap option to buying new tungsten darts simply because of wear. Scrapping or giving away favorite darts is foolish. Buying new darts whenever the urge hits proves costly. Big changes in a dart's weight or shape can also badly upset your game.

Ensure changing darts is right, before buying. Try another player's similar darts or test at a dart shop. I learned the hard (costly) way not to <u>blindly</u> buy darts from catalogs or through the mail. Buying darts solely by price or looks is a no-no! Credit is rare if the darts dash your hopes. Often, I almost gave away decent darts to get back some return on my investment.

120 **RESPECT OTHER PLAYERS:** Never take any rival lightly. She may appear an easy win. Take care!

A few big scoring darts (even strays) can put you in a deep hole. Players may look new to the game, but appearances or odd styles can mislead you. None is reason to get careless. You may even run into a teetotaler (like me). That 'old timer' you are playing could be the author! You may win, but will earn it.

Keep a positive manner while never easing off in matches. You may regret not treating a rival with due respect. Play your normal game against all comers. I see many able dartists lose because they let up playing weaker shooters.

Take great care not to insult an opponent(s)—very easy to do. Blowing him away, the first leg, do not think: "He doesn't belong at this level of play. I don't even have to try to win, etc." These ideas may or may not be true. Many better players do blow hot and cold. He could just be having an off night. If kicked when down, you may spur him to react. Simply finish the match quickly, without comment or deed.

What injures a darter's pride? For one, unless you always

throw the first dart at the double bull going in, DO NOT after a blowout! The message heard is "I can easily beat you." Possibly! However, I can vouch, most will take it like a stinging slap. Angering a rival, this way, can goad him to extra effort. Another big no-no is to start throwing darts off-handed.

An average darter, instead of forfeiting, agrees to play CRICKET shorthanded, allowing you a shot at a round of nine. Unless you should get that chance, do not go out of your way to point her. You are adding an insult to injury. You will tally enough points from fallouts without trying. She may never again give you a no-pressure chance at a trophy. Should you have an all-star throw (after piling up points) she could decide simply to forfeit and erase your feat!

Be careful with words too. Snide remarks to (or from) a mate or fan, about easy wins or the level of play, can be fatal. Make a point to disown rude comments from others' mouths. Tell them to stifle it—mates also!

A ROBOT: In theory, every body motion should be perfect when throwing darts. A robot, with powers | **121** | equal to the human brain, would always be flawless. Setting up to throw, act as though you are a robot. Do not be a killjoy. Yet, do not hamper yourself with sloppy habits.

| **122** | **ROUTINES:** During practice, follow some system. Methods need not be rigid, or without change. However, DO set some goals. The two league games are '01' and CRICKET. Many dart players prefer one of these games to the other.

Better players train to play both games well, even when partial to one. Slant your routines toward the game you least enjoy. I cannot tell you how. My basic routine and thinking follow.

I play decent '01' and merely so-so CRICKET games. I start by throwing 20 darts or so with my off-hand. Then using my dart hand hit three bulls. Trying to improve my CRICKET game, I score on the six triples 15 through 20. Hitting triples is great '01' *AND* CRICKET game practice. Then, I hit three more bulls.

Next, I hit all the doubles, 1 through 20, Double bull too, finishing with a Double 1 and three more bulls. If possible, I repeat this cycle or play a few '01' or CRICKET games. Often, I vary my routine or shuffle for variety. I finish my routine every time, even when it seems a chore. You need not follow my routine or anyone else's. Yet, do put some logic behind practice methods. You gain little by simply throwing at random.

RUSHING: Throwing a dart before your mind and body are ready is asking for trouble. Instead, develop a | 123 | steady rhythm coupled with a smooth unbroken throw. Set up fully before every shot, and then lock into your rhythm. NEVER RUSH A SHOT!

Your tempo should remain uniform. Throwing faster or slower than normal upsets your natural rhythm, making playing your best darts a task. Do not think you must throw slowly. Play at a speed you feel at ease with and does the job.

S-A-D: The feeling after losing a game because you shot at a wrong target. Avoid getting down on yourself. | 124 | On occasion, we all make silly mistakes. As with other errors, use this one to learn Darts finer points. Becoming upset at making errors, you will simply repeat them.

Having a mental lapse, at the line, simply not knowing your next move, recall the letters' S-A-D! Letters meaning STOP, ASK and DECIDE!

STOP, means exactly that. Never throw a dart without a precise target. Realize that your target may not be one | ◀12 4 | that another player would shoot at there. You may make an error in judgment. A 'mistake' is often simply the choice made, based on what you know about your skills. Consider other views when heard. NEVER ignore faultfinders. Learn to smile and accept criticism with a grain of salt. You will improve faster.

For instance, with 25 left, most darters go for a 9 to leave 16. Should you dislike the 9, but feel you can hit a 17 (leaving 8) try. With two darts in hand, 17 is a better shot with a rival about to finish. Missing 9 often leaves you odd, with only a single dart left.

No one can double out with a single dart from an odd

| **Mark Holland (MARKO)** |

number! A miss at 17 may leave you even. True that number may not prove great for doubling out, but you at least get a chance! Players weak on 9 may throw at the four abutting odd wedges at the board's bottom. A single on any of those wedges at least ensures a game-winning attempt.

Personal liking or opinions aside, times arise when you truly cannot decide where to shoot next. Your mind simply goes totally blank! Your worst move, here, is going ahead and shooting, without thought. Haste gains little and risks too much.

One reason for hurrying is not wanting to break your rhythm, which offers small comfort after you give away a game. Remember, even when feeling foolish standing at the line gathering your wits, winning is your first aim. Never rush off a shot. Take all the time needed—within reason, of course!

ASK, the next logical step: A chalker must tell you the score when asked, but cannot volunteer help. You could get wrong information, though you and she both drawing blanks at once is unlikely. However, the responsibility for all errors is yours.

Look closely at the last few scores. Your brain, seeing an error, may use a memory lapse to gain your attention. Stop and ask for facts from another source. Breaking a trance, **DECIDE!**

AVOIDING SETBACKS: If a practice session is going **VERY** badly, STOP! Yet, do not quit each time you face problems. Facing and solving problems is one big | 125 | reason for practice. However, at times, going on is unwise. You could badly bruise your ego.

Mental pain added to anger could easily drain faith in your darting ability. Going on, for even a short time, may hurt you. Rebuilding poise could take months.

NEVER throw darts when angry or out-of-control in practice or league play. Never! I broke this rule twice in thirteen plus years. Both times I wished I could have crawled under a rug or vanished. Once, I nearly hit an eight-month pregnant woman keeping the score. The other time, I looked and played like a fool.

What should you do when totally losing your cool? When

Chet's Diner   **Ron Gebo**

you sense anger rising, crush it quickly. Unable to do so, make any excuse to stop and get away from the area. Say you need to use the rest room, refill or get a drink—unless that __IS__ the problem. Hide bad feelings from all players. Regain control of emotions. Sit! With no outlet, breathe deeply, before throwing.

No good can ever come from playing in anger. Losing control often brands you a sore loser (even if winning) and someone to avoid. You can easily damage darts, board and people (you included) with wild throws.

126 **SHAFTS:** Shafts come in as many, maybe more, shapes and materials as flights. New styles appear constantly. When perfecting a straight dart (an art), find the best shafts and flights for you. Erase minor problems by fine-tuning your setup. Avoid changing your grip, stroke or throw. Following are the pointers to your best setup:

♣ Darts should fly smoothly with no wobble.

♣ A dart's arc must work with your throw.

♣ Darts should enter the board at a correct angle, not veering off line.

♣ Too long a combination (for you) is a hazard to your face and eyes.

♣ A combination cannot be too short to avoid its hitting finger(s) upon release.   **◀126**

♣ A setup must reduce robin-hooding and bouncing off other darts.

♣ A dart's surface should show no gaps or bulges to snag on, deflect darts or irritate your grip.

Metal shafts often loosen at the worst possible time. Other materials also work loose. Most darters simply ignore such 'small' points. Minor points can add up to big edges if you face each and make changes.

A shaft length, weight, (or both) can make for drastic

Richard Gigliotti (GIGS)

changes in your dart's accuracy. I am still struggling to find my 'right' shaft. I know the best weight, form and flight shape for my dart. To date, the correct shaft eludes me. My dart lands low, one throw out of three with shafts giving an ideal arc and angle. Shafts giving greater accuracy made my darts wobble, striking the board so badly they often fell to the floor.

[Eureka! I recently solved my landing low problem. The answer was moving my middle finger off the top of the dart point. My fingertip side now *lightly* touches the point. A mere 1/4-inch move—but oh the difference! No more fighting and total dart control.]

You might lose a game or match when a shaft loosens or falls off causing your dart to go astray. If this happens, you feel helpless.

The small 'O' rings sold to prevent this nagging problem may make it worse. Tightening your shaft, the rubber often bulges or leaves gaps. Uneven surfaces bother fingers or, worse, may snag a dart point to cause bounceouts or off-target throws. So-called small accidents affect many game outcomes. The perfect answer is SHAFTITE™—see BONUSES. The peace of mind gained provides an added edge.

| 127 |

BROKEN SHAFTS: All shafts break, even metal ones, always seeming to snap off flush, or below, at the worst time. What can you do? Short of carrying a spare dart(s), you could try using friends' darts. Yet, the chance of finding a set you feel at ease with is slim to none. You could try borrowing one dart. Yet, matching a dart's shape and weight is unlikely, making a worse situation, throwing you off badly.

Your best answer is removing the broken piece, putting in a new shaft—carry spares! One method is to ask someone to hold the dart firmly while you turn out the stub using two darts with very sharp points. With a nonmetallic stub, dig the points in at opposite sides and twist it out—often quite easy.

Removal may be harder when a broken piece is metal, not too difficult though. You seldom deal with wholly smooth surfaces. Get points into rough spots, or dig some, then with a

| *Chris Manos* | *Marlboro Fish & Game* |

firm grip, remove the piece. NOTE! Dart suppliers now sell a tool for this job.

| 128 | **SHOES:** An excellent pair of shoes is your best darting aide. Buying correct shoes, is a wise purchase as nothing else eases sore feet. You must feel totally comfortable at the line. Buy the best affordable shoes.

One vital point, dart shoes need firm bottoms. Solid soles are your stance's base, thus your game. Wearing loafers, sneakers or other soft-soled shoes makes you wobbly. Your body then rocks with every shot. You cannot stand unmoving with an unstable base. Small movements will cause perfect throws to miss. Start on the right foot. Wear proper shoes.

I throw some 90% of my practice from THE PLATFORM™ in soft-soled shoes. Then, in matches I am rock solid in my DART shoes. For a real workout, I also practice with both eyes closed.

SHOOTING THE BULL: An unusual practice method you should use to improve your bullseye | 129 | scoring skills. Throw only at the bullseye, not the wedge you usual use for scoring.

Now, with 57 or 65 left in a match, you should not hesitate in shooting for a single bull. Hitting 25 leaves you 32 or 40. Both are excellent outs. Any miss, including a double bull, still allows you a shot to even your score or hopefully the win. With only two darts left, no other way is open for a shot at the Double 16 or Double 20.

Once at ease with shooting the bullseye, you should feel more confident going for a bull when needed. Shooting for the double bull to win is a very safe shot as it is highly unlikely you will bust. Hitting the double bull to win is extremely exciting and very reassuring to any player even a Pro.

You merit great satisfaction in accomplishing this feat. This out is seen more often than you might think. I promise you will never forget the first time you take out the double bull.

| 130 | **SLEEP:** Being well rested is a big factor going into any match, before an important dart match—vital. Reaching the Pro's a good night's sleep can often make the difference between winning and losing. Yet, nerves can make

sleeping just before tournaments difficult if not impossible.

Take care not to build up too big a sleep deficit prior to critical matches. With rare exceptions, we all need a solid 8 to 9 hours sleep nightly for peak performance. When you fall below **_your_** sleep needs a deficit starts. Once the lack reaches a certain point, which varies individually, you cannot expect to perform up to par, never mind beyond.

How to test yourself for a sleep deficit? Each day, about 8 to 10 hours after rising you will experience a (normal) period of reduced awareness before getting a second wind, so to speak, to carry you through to bedtime. Thus, if you normally wake around 6AM, at 2 or 3PM (about an hour or two after your midday meal) you should be at your lowest point of the day. Once knowing when this is, lie down then and try to nap.

Somehow, check how long it takes you to fall asleep. Falling off in 5 minutes or less you have an extreme sleep deficit. Between 5 and 10 minutes means a large deficit. 10 to 15 minutes is borderline and 15 to 20 normal. Get up after 20 minutes if awake, as you have no deficit. The worse your sleep deficit the less responsive you are mentally and physically. See how this can badly affect your game. Get enough sleep!

Are you sleepy or groggy during the day? Do you snore, are depressed or have other persistent symptoms that doctors cannot seem to diagnose?

There are many sleep ailments that (being asleep) you may be totally unaware of and, unfortunately, few physicians are trained to detect. At the very least, have a spouse or friend watch while you sleep. If they see anything unusual, have a sleep specialist test you for any sleep disorders, as soon as possible.

A Personal Note: You may think me an alarmist, but we lost a healthy 36-year-old son to a sleep disorder. Namely; sleep apnea. Unable to breathe properly, his heart (weakened by a years-old illness) gave out and he died in his sleep. Again, I strongly urge you to see a specialist with any of these symptoms.

SLUMPS: Give your brain pep talks, especially when throwing below par. NEVER get down on yourself! Nothing harms you more. Try smiling until your face hurts. Shrug off horrid slumps—easily said, for many,

131

difficult. We all go through slumps. Now is the time for much practice. REPETITION, REPETITION, REPETITION! Throwing more often improves the chance of finding flaws.

A slump is a Dart's rite-of-passage to better things. Those who give up, or give in, never IMPROVE. I know of no darter, average or pro, who never faced at least one horrible career slump. Sticking with it and getting beyond this hump is a necessity to improving at Darts. Part of the maturing process all darters must endure. During a slump is the best time for trying new ideas. I doubt you could damage your game further now. Many novel ideas are in this book, for exactly that reason. One 'absurd' notion may be exactly what you need to get your game on track.

One trick is to stop throwing for three or four days, throwing perfect mental darts instead. Resuming, fit methods with those 'seen' in your mind. Defects, unnoticed while in your slump, may now appear clear. Maybe you were too close to the problem. Long slumps test any dart player's self-control and esteem.

It is a struggle. You now see if a dartist is just a decent shooter Or a TEAM player too. Winners keep supporting and rooting for their team. Winners never complain when the captain cuts back their games played. Realize a captain's concern is, rightfully, the team's welfare. The captain hopes your slump is very short too. Yet, the team must come first.

◀131 Teams need all players at peak form to compete. Never react badly should you sit; though you may be the team's top gun. Swallow your pride, work for the team's welfare. Tell your captain when feeling sub par **BEFORE** she makes up the match roster. The captain can decide when you play. Never excuse a poor night, **AFTER** losing two or three points, because you did not feel 'up' to playing. This is a selfish act and not thinking of the team.

Volunteer for whatever the team needs done, especially when in a slump. For example, chalk (keep the score) for an entire match, even though you dislike the chore. Keep your eyes open and stay impartial. You could learn some new details.

Bob Couture

Be a TEAM player. Become your teams number one fan and morale booster (except when chalking). A positive attitude on your part will work wonders for the team. Instead of dragging the team down with constant griping, your loyal spirit inspires and lifts teammates. Staying positive, helps your team carry the load until you regain your form.

As a league captain for years, I assure you these rare players are team assets. I would love carrying a roster of those players, whatever their darting skills. Such a team would soon earn respect in any league, at all skill levels. A captain's job is difficult, thankless at times. Make every effort possible to ease that burden.

132 **PLAYING SMART DARTS:** Fact, you win or lose all '01' games (if required) on doubles. Failing to double in or out, even the world's best scorer cannot win '01' games. Failing to play smart Darts, you can hit those doubles and still lose too often. Close to going out, you can lose by throwing one dart at a wrong target—especially true from 60 downward.

A sound rule is to avoid throwing at a wedge if hitting its triple busts you or leaves an unwanted number. Deciding you must play this wedge always favor the end nearest its double.

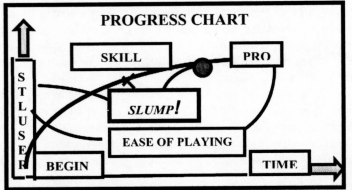

PROGRESS CHART

RESULTS

SKILL

PRO

SLUMP!

EASE OF PLAYING

BEGIN

TIME

How to read the chart above: Going from amateur to pro takes time. Naturals may get there quickly while others (most of us) never reach this point. No real end exists in the result curve if you keep working to improve. Do not let slumps get to you!

Beginners most often do much better than reason says they should. Why! They simply do not know how hard throwing a dart is and their brain works as it should. Once novices try to improve, problems begin. Learning to throw darts right is a long and winding route, with unlike turns for each of us. The Natural meets few hills or turns. Amateurs see little else. They are often totally lost, with accidents and detours!

I, for one, made every mistake you can imagine—learning so much along the way! The chart clearly shows what to expect, between now and the next level, in your darting career. Knowing slumps will come helps in getting past them.

The mastery of technique's curve is not smooth, as shown. A blowup at any spot, in its arc, would look similar to the total chart, a series of bumps, like a toothed wheel. Bogging down (at any point) is easy when one becomes too content there.

The ball is where better dart careers' peak. Not getting beyond average (the + mark) Darts can still provide lifelong pleasure.

Making a 'wire shot' is going for the center of two wedges to reach a makeable double safely. With even scores from 42 to 58 and two (or three) darts in hand, use the trio of side-by-side wedges, the 4—18, 6—10 and 8—16. Facing a hard double, for you, these three sets of wedges can prove godsends. Going from an odd number to a double, remember the 7—19—3—17 wedges. If you hit dividing wires often, you do not need this method, but it is always available.

Use those three even pairs with 14, 18, 22, 26, 30, 34, or 38 (the odd number doubles) with two or three

◄132

darts left. Missing ANY odd-numbered double usually busts or leaves you odd. Uneven, you will need at least one dart to even up, another (IF handy) to win.

Many players, without thinking twice, throw at odd-numbered doubles. If you are unable to hit a double in one or two shots, every time, this practice is not playing smart Darts.

Avoid finishing with three points. Three is a killer! Down to six points with one dart left, go for a single 2 or 4. Hitting a single 3, trying for Double 3, is trouble unless holding a dart(s) to correct. With one dart, bust purposely, unless sure of hitting Double 1 later. Caution! Ensure busting. Do not throw wildly.

Leaving six can prove fatal to a game's outcome. You must go for Double 3, on occasion, to win. Yet, this is often a losing move. Avoid Double 3 whenever possible. I see darters going for Double 3 too often in bouts. Okay when hurting only you, but not if your team suffers.

Players too often go for Double 3 when their opponent is not in yet! Wasting too many shots, trying to win, stubborn shooters eventually lose. Many darters turn right around, going for Double 3 again next time six remains. Stubborn darters look for ways to lose. Meeting with problems doubling in or out, change doubles, fast. Change! Even if that double is your pet.

Somehow winding up with three while owning a big lead and leery about hitting Double 1, go on as follows: Ignore all other darts once hitting your single one. Throw below the

Chez Chesnulavich   **Missy Chesnulavich**

dartboard or simply drop your dart(s). For safety sake though, simply walk up and remove your dart(s). No rule says you MUST throw. However a rule does state your throw is over once touching a dart in the board.

◀132 Then you must (merely) contend with Double 1. You may dislike Double 1, but certainly need it from three, regardless. This method is easier than making two shots in one turn. Try for an easy way!

The obvious answer is, avoid leaving three. Sidestep, by looking ahead before throwing your third dart. Then, only a bounceout or wild final dart can strand you at three. Naturally, there comes a time you must hit Double 1. Blame could be yours or a partner. With practice, you can hit Double 1 when needed.

One trap in CRICKET is running up the score, not closing bulls to win. Occasionally you must build a cushion, but avoid routinely piling up points. Putting bulls off can cost you games. Face the situation. Close the bulls! Avoiding them makes hitting bulls later, more difficult. We once won a play-off game with 17 unanswered bulls while they ran up the score.

Pay close attention. How many hits do you need to close a wedge? Not closing an open number or throwing at a closed one is costly. You may need that wasted dart(s) to win at the end.

STANCE: The handling of the body after placing feet is your stance. Working up, checkpoint one is the ◀13 3 knee joint. Keep your knees relaxed, at ease, not stiff. Lock knees (lightly) when working on licking flaws like dipping or tiptoeing.

Keep the body stable. Avoid rotating your hips. Most darters lean forward at their waist, shifting weight onto the front leg, under the throwing arm. Yet, I see a few better players use their off-leg with decent results. Stand erect, unless this throws you off balance. To cut swaying, stand at an angle to the board, twisting a little at the waist.

Place your shoulders, like feet, anywhere from square with the board or angled up to 90 degrees. Avoid angles that make you use muscles other than the shoulder's to hold up the arm.

Angel Chevere

Flex only arm muscles.

Grasp the muscles under the arm, front and back, with your off-hand while throwing. The shoulder angle is correct when feeling little or (ideally) no tension in those muscles. You need not throw with shoulders in any fixed position. Ideal position is simply the point of least muscle usage. Never change a stance you feel at ease with. Your brain simply uses other muscles.

Keep head and eyes square with the board. How you manage this is not crucial. Turn head and body as one or just the head alone. With both eyes square you ideally look right at double bull. To shoot at another target, move your eyes, not your head. If very short, or tall, tilt your head to move eyes easily, but avoid sideways. Try bending up or down at the waist.

No matter how you set up, let your brain take over at the last moment. Then, throw the dart.

◀13
4

REPLACING FIXED STEEL POINTS: This is much like pulling teeth. Done correctly, a messy job is complete. If not, the task only gets worse. Do not try pulling points unless you are handy with tools. Replacing a point is major dart surgery.

First, clamp the dart's tip securely in a bench vise. Point downward. Leaving enough space between its body and vise to insert a (small) V-notched lever.

Then, push down sharply, popping the point out cleanly. Clean the dart body's hole with a sharp point. Test the new point for fit. The point must go in smoothly all the way. Check that the point does not bind. Remove snags by reaming the hole carefully, by hand, using a 3/32-inch drill bit.

Ensure a proper fit for the point. Then, clamp the dart's body (wrapped in a rag for protection) gently in a vise, hole upward. Put a drop of instant glue in the hole, at once; push the new point in all the way. For now, ignore any excess glue.

Let glue dry one hour before using the dart. Scrape excess glue off with a razor blade or sharp knife. Carefully remove all marks on the dart using a fine file or emery cloth. Done right, new points will last years.

With constant use, original steel points may need changing in as little as six months. By then, even though still straight, points may wear down as much as 1/4-inch. Wear results from keeping points sharp after bounceouts and the sisal fibers wearing action. Cement floors are murder on darts. Avoid playing on cement if at all possible.

If you replace a point because of wear, breakage or bending use one of stainless steel. Stainless is much ◀134 stronger, wearing down slower. After replacing, compare the new point's length with the other two darts. The newly pointed dart probably now weighs a tad more. If the other tips vary 1/8-inch or more in length, replace all three points.

Better dart shops carry new points. Again, stainless steel points are best as regular steel points wear down faster and bend more easily. Some shops will install new points, for a fee.

◀13 5 **STRESS:** It comes in two forms, good and bad. Finding harmful stress is easy. Simply worry about what can go wrong. You will see a great deal. Build useful stress with long hours of practice. The best fact about stress is the positive replaces the negative.

An essential growth element! Positive stress is a sure way to improve at Darts. No stress (in practice) means little growth. During stressful times, focus on what you want, or must do. Vital! Relax every chance you get, even briefly. Frequent stress, and then relaxation is how we grow! Each time stress becomes easier to handle.

Play practice games you can lose. Losing, or the fear of losing, causes ALL negative stress.

Stress-full routines! Play '01' or CRICKET games against yourself. Allowing X darts to complete. Failing, you lose. Keep lowering the total darts needed to finish. A game called 27 is very stressful. Starting with 27 points, throw three darts at each double. Begin at D-1, working in order toward D-20. Add a double's point value for each hit, deducting for three misses. Example, add 52 for two Double 13's or deduct 26 for none. The trick, end with points NOT merely finishing.

Another game building tension is No-Miss Doubles. Again,

Three G's Sportsbar   *Troy C. Foskett*

work from D-1 toward D-20. Hitting a double, move to the next higher one. The catch is if a scoring dart lands anywhere besides an aimed for double you must return to the last one. I advise setting a time limit, then quit. Anger can eat at you, causing negative stress. Simply getting to where you can deal with feelings is progress.

Mix practice up now and then. Variety spurs interest, so you do drill.

STROKE OR ARM MOTION: Throwing, are you flagging a train down or gently drying nails? Most darters fall between those arm motion extremes. No one form is ideal for all. One's form can change daily when trying to find what works best. Changes can prove so slow that they remain unseen. Pros come closest to a pure fixed stroke. Experts also stay alert to improving. Their changes are smaller, not obvious.

I can hear you now. "You must be kidding! I simply grip my dart then throw at the target. You're making a big deal out of nothing, what's the difference?" None, if 100 percent happy now. Throwing perfectly, you will not gain until refining motion. Your stroke is THE KEY!

"Okay, so what can I do with my stroke? You keep saying my game should stay natural. If I make changes, won't that harm my game? Besides, I can't think of one fix I could try!" True, new ways may upset until you train your brain. Those periods are joyfully short for positive steps though. The brain learns quickly. Use any idea making its job easier.

However, the brain is lazy, seldom finding better ways on its own. Go with what the brain knows or retrain it. Plant new ideas with your mind, otherwise the brain keeps using what worked before.

◄136 YOUR MIND IS MASTER! Tell your brain what you want then relax, letting it work. Talk to the brain as though your desire is a fact. The brain cannot tell fact from fancy. With total faith in your bidding, it grants wishes! A well-trained brain obeys all commands.

As for changes, I asked that question for many years. Below is a short list of those I found (not in any order). I could list more, but these should keep you busy. Finishing this list, unearth others. A big secret! Never stop refining or feel totally happy with your stroke.

SOME STROKE OPTIONS

GRIP? <u>FOR MORE DETAILS</u> See Articles. #71, 72 & 73.

HAND SPEED? See #77.

FOLLOW-THROUGH? See #46 & 64.

WHERE SHOULD MY STROKE BEGIN AND END? See #46.

BODY MOVEMENTS? See #112.

ARM TRAVEL DISTANCE? Often a tough nut to crack. You may need a long or short arm sweep. Although a longer swing takes your mind off throwing it might not work well. A simple flip shot is deadly, if able to focus on the target, not your hand.

KEEP WRIST STIFF OR PIVOT? Loose, or with purpose. Snap the dart or a smooth release?

WHERE DO I PIVOT, at the fingers, wrist, elbow, shoulders, my upper body or the entire body using waist or knees?

THROWING MOTION? Smooth all the way or with a slight pause? For some, pausing at the stroke's back increases accuracy and causes a smoother jerk-free delivery.

THROW EASY OR HARD? Your call! Easy, is best to manage.

A LOOSE OR RIGID MOTION?

AIM OR NO?

FLOATING OR RIGID ELBOW?

Many options exist. Any one may prove A KEY!

STUBBORNNESS: Playing a board wisely is basic Dart's skill. Know what YOU can and cannot do with the darts. Throwing at a hard target (for you), with better ways plus time, could turn many wins into loses. Playing a foolish shot (for you) on another's say so, is also asking to lose.

◀13
7

For example, with 18 left in '01', I rarely shoot for Double 9 holding more than one dart. Others often scold me for not trying. However, I know my chances of hitting Double 9 approach zero!

I hit all doubles (Double 9s included) every day, in practice. Yet in thirteen plus years of twice weekly league play, I only recently made that double for the FIRST time! Then, (in a play-off match) I went for the win because I held only <u>one dart</u> with my opponent at 32. I saw no choice and got lucky!

Avoiding double 9 is not a failure on my part. I simply know the odds are slim, of hitting it. At that point recovering quickly from a miss is difficult. If I get stubborn, trying to win, I usually regret my act. Too often, I needlessly lose the leg or match.

Small points play big roles in throwing winning Darts. So remember, use your head to play smart Darts.

138 **TEAM STRATEGIES:** An article for, the often overlooked, team captain. Having never served you cannot know how thankless this job can be. Dart players have big egos and satisfying everyone, whether pros or beginners, impossible. Never become captain of any team with even one member who cannot or will not abide by your word. You should not be a dictator but all must obey or the team will fail. Even on a team run by consent of the majority, the captain's word is final.

Once in charge, you must prove yourself worthy. As captain, you need to learn everyone's traits, such as, temperament, cooperation and tenacity. These are often more vital than darting skills especially in team play. Teams need time to reach their potential. They must learn to work together like a well-oiled machine.

Your best darter may be a disaster in team games. Your least capable (real or no) can be the glue needed in these matches. The anchor's skill may be so-so but she thrives under pressure. The strongest team is often a group of average, unselfish players. Regardless of skill, selfish darters are not assets. Personal conflicts make some pairings impossible.

I cannot know the format of your league. However, common practice is to put better players at the matches' end. That is fine. Usually! However, how often do one or two points decide a season? Give serious thought to winning extra points with a little lineup juggling. For instance, the other team's anchor shoots like

Joanne P. Maus

a pro and rarely loses. Why waste your best against him or her? Put your weakest shooter up there. Why? Several reasons, instead of losing two points you may only lose one. In addition, your weak shooter will get in some quality playing time (this is how they improve). Let them know you do not expect a win and they may relax and do just that. I see it happen all too often.

Do not rule out any grouping without trying it a few times. I see many odd couples or trios who prove ◀138 almost unbeatable once paired. The only answer to why is often "chemistry". There is no logical reason, but you will never know without trying. For instance, I am a terrible Cricket player yet the captain paired me with one particular teammate. On paper, we did not figure to win a match. We had an unbeaten season.

A caution! Never let the other team know when you expect to play shorthanded. Then, mix up where you play short. One trap is playing your best shooter alone in Cricket. Two on one, even a pro will struggle to beat average players. Best strategy is to concede one Cricket match and fight for the others.

Always think logically about a lineup. Do not blindly play every match the same. A few extra points over a season can mean first place instead of second or gaining a playoff spot.

139 THINK: Once below 100, you are within a few darts of doubling out to win. With odd numbers left, STOP AND THINK! Few players run into problems with even numbers, but use care there, too. Pausing may be the turning point, assuring a win in steel-tipped matches needing a final double.

Ignoring double bull, you can win, from any odd (or even) number from 80 down with two single ◀139 numbers and a double. Note, considering 25 a 'single' number, 81, 83 & 85 obey this rule too. Single bull is also the percentage shot for 82 and 84. Above 85, you must hit at least one triple (or two doubles) to win with two or three darts.

Example: With 23 left and in a big hurry, I shot for single 15 to leave Double 4. Twice I hit a 15, busting with the second dart. The third time I hit Double 15 to bust. I did not get another chance!

Not a poor shot choice, for me! I often get in on Double 4,

feeling at ease there. Later, I saw my error. The best option was the 7-19 wedges. They offered my best chance for a win. Side by side numbers! I could land one or two wedges to the right, leaving an out shot. Hitting 7 or 19 leaves me with 16 (Double 8) or 4 (Double 2), both excellent outs. Facing like problems, ask three questions BEFORE throwing!

ONE, at what double(s) should I throw? **YOUR** easiest double(s), if possible! Get into the 32-16-8-4-2 series (or other favorite cycle) as high as possible. Avoid leaving odd-number doubles, 38 or 34 for example. Without another choice or short on time, go right at all doubles including double bull (50). Any chance is superior to none.

TWO, Can I get there quickly and safely. What if I miss! Have I enough darts? With time, play safely. Going for, say triple 13 (39) then Double 16 (32) with 71 left is a dramatic finish, without dispute. Yet, this is not a SAFE combo, with a rival far from a game shot.

THREE, what is the smallest odd number I must hit to reach a makeable double? For a number larger than 19, can I get there in two singles with a shot at winning on my third dart? If not, should I go for a double or triple (how close is your opponent)?

If unable to memorize those three questions, note them on a small card. Laminate or keep your card in a clear plastic holder. USE it!

140 **THINKING:** Avoid thinking while throwing! A mind's normal state is chaos. With mind chatter going on, you cannot throw your best darts. Stop what you are doing if unwanted thoughts enter the mind. Delay throwing until dealing with distractions. The best thing to do is to redirect your mind.

For instance, looking at the target, focus on keeping your back foot's heel touching the floor—sensing pressure, throw. The mind cannot raise random thoughts while working on a direct order.

Getting this method down pat, you need no reminder to focus elsewhere. You see little trouble later in erasing mental

Kenny Seidenberg

images. Faced with problems (personal or otherwise) so pressing you cannot clear your mind, simply sit out a match, if possible!

141 **THROWAWAY DARTS:** have you seen darters who bust, become upset, then throw away their other dart(s)? It amazed me how often those throws hit the just-missed target. This happens far too frequently to be accidental. I think the brain is showing that if allowed, it could make the shot.

AFTER losing, do not throw darts at that double you were unable to hit. Hitting your target then, even on the first dart, means nothing and can only upset . You cannot compare this shot with those thrown under pressure. Always doing this could lead to steering (the dart) with every shot and destroying your faith.

Thinking you would have won, given another chance, is false. Why ADD torment to losing? Avoid doing this to yourself. Simply forget a loss; go to the next game. EACH GAME IS A NEW CHALLENGE. PREVIOUS WINS OR LOSSES MEAN NOTHING.

TOO HIGHLY PLACED: You may start, by **142** chance, on a too-highly-placed team. If your team moves up the rivalry may prove an ordeal, rarely winning. Decide! Hang in there, improving skills or join a lower-position team?

How will you fare? You often prove nervous, giving the other side an easy win. It seems you always pair with their hottest or best player, never winning or even coming close. Make your first goal getting at least a shot at winning ONE leg. At first, you seem, at best, forever one dart short of a win. Your best shots bounce out or deflect off previous darts.

Stay in there! With skill and desire, you will slip into gear and start getting your shots at winning. Then, you are off and running!

◄142 Realize that you will lose many games starting too high, or moving up too quickly, in league play. With grit plus tolerant team members I think the sink or swim method is best and often only method for some players to improve. Moving up quick is difficult! You must come up to the higher

The Hitchin' Post

level quality of play, fast. Do not feel shocked if teammates lose patience, should you not improve rapidly. Holding a team down, mates may resent you.

Play against better players, but avoid competing totally out of your league. Competing is enjoying some chance of winning, even if wins are few. With no chance of winning, you become upset and bitter.

Persist! Practice every day. You WILL improve. Know progress may not go as fast as wished. All skills require some natural talent to reach higher levels no matter how much you drill. With that gift, you must nevertheless practice faithfully to stay sharp. Experts spend hours every day staying on top of their game.

Return to a level that you win roughly half the time. Stay there until winning more often. Two reasons for moving down. One, excess anxiety is unfair to you. You no longer enjoy Darts. Two, the team cannot find their ideal competitive level. Enjoy playing with equally skilled darters, more. Play at your skill level and enjoy.

Avoid playing below your skill level, unless you want to win often, playing a team's star. Most darters find winning easily boring, as little challenge exists. You do not help opponents either. Capable players may give up on Darts before given a chance to develop skills. Darts needs new blood to grow and stay strong.

UPBEAT: End every practice with a double, triple

143

or bull. You can walk away feeling upbeat after a so-so session. Forget all missed shots and recall only hits, though scarce at first. Mind training helps you focus, greatly building one's ego and confidence.

Now, if you miss a shot, in a match, you can live with it and continue. Work at delivering one perfect dart each throw, ignoring the rest. Think 'this dart is THE one' every time. Reach this goal and you will become a great dart player. You can do it! Tell your brain often, "Every day in every positive way I improve!" You will!

UPS AND DOWNS: Wild swings in game results **144** can be amazing. Within a few weeks, I played in two awesome final-leg games. First, I won a game from 200 using six darts (including a one and a miss). With my rival at 32, I hit 60, 60, and 1 for 121 leaving 79. My opponent hit 16, 16 for a bust. I hit 57, miss and Double 11 to win.

A few weeks later the outcome reversed. With 170 left and my competitor at 160, I hit 116, leaving 54, an excellent position. Yet, I never got a shot at winning as he closed with 60, 60 Double 20! I later saw him beat the current top USA professional.

Most players would agree the win was a plus, the loss a debit. I felt right about both games. Surely, I earned no shame for my effort. I felt proud sharing in a match that my opponent needed a plaque winning effort to win. Enjoy Darts to the utmost! Look for positives in every match. At the very least, the other side is happy.

FUNNEL VISION: Your target may often seem **145** covered by an unseen cone with its pointed end facing you. That shape deflects every dart coming close and a great way of building a negative outlook.

A trick is to view a target from the cone's big end. Mentally, cut off its tip and turn the cone around making a funnel. Then, delivering your darts, simply imagine throwing into the opening to hit your target.

We all play Darts with some mental image. For best results, use your thoughts positively.

WORRYING: Never dwell on mistakes made while **146** playing Darts. Letting errors gnaw, you risk being unable to make the next throw fearing another boner. Every dart match is a series of errors, physical or mental, large and small. Even experts rarely throw like a machine. ANY perfect game is BIG NEWS.

Do not put yourself down for every mistake—that is foolish thinking. A great way to view errors is that the brain is guiding you to what IT wants, despite your mind's efforts. Learn to 'go

Billy Bigelow (BINK)

with the flow'. A meddling mind causes too many errors.

Your brain knows exactly what you need, a certain number, triple or bull. Your mind intrudes with ◀146 thoughts like "I can't hit double bull" or "what can I do when I miss?" Other bad thoughts "don't hit a one" or "I'll never hit a double." Get my drift? These are all negative, self-fulfilling ideas. Like someone telling you not to think of pink elephants. Pop—there they are!

Ignore physical or mental lapses. If you make an error or miss an easy shot, forget it. Go right on with your next shot. Exceptions are errors in good sense or strategy. Still, examine all slips AFTER you finish, not during a match! Weigh mental mistake(s), learning from your blunders, filing answers away for the future. Forget mistakes—remember fixes.

Think positive, ALWAYS! Realize making mistakes is human. Never think of giving up, taking what comes. On the contrary, simply throw your best darts. NEVER concede defeat! Simply bear errors or lost games. Learn what you can from a mistake. Then, at once, wipe that slip forever from memory. If you lose, while playing your best, think, "it was fate" and move ahead. Your rival simply played the board better 'this' match, earning a win. Never expose yourself to undue stress.

All your mind's effort should aim to reduce the brains work. A player's 'ultimate dartist' is the brain, their success secret. Failures are the minds, for not setting up the body right, for the brain to use.

Our brains work perfectly. Otherwise, we could not exist. Any error by the brain would prove fatal to your body. Once you see this, the value of using proper method's in practice is clear. Work on all parts of your game, watching details. Polish each facet.

Realize, perfect darts, when achieved, are brief. The closer you near an ideal, the easier the brain's task. Your 'ultimate dartist' can reach great heights. Never make your brain struggle with false thinking, frequent body movements or stroke changes. Develop what works *__for you__* to an art.

| *Bill Thomson* | *Ernie Desabre* |

105

WRIST SHOOTING: Harder to master than the catapult delivery, wrist shooting is a great throwing system. Yet, avoid this method until in complete control of your game. Mastering this system, the rewards are many. Wrist action speeds up your dart, giving a flatter arc. This yields tighter, more accurate, groups. This cuts your arm motion, back and forth, so you need not move forward as fast. Less motion allows for a more controlled throw.

Timing must be precise when using a wrist shot. Bring your wrist back to its final, locked position, before starting the arm motion. Position your wrist, then pull your forearm back one or two inches (with the wrist) to trigger the throw. Blend the two motions into one.

Darters who set up with their forearm upright, or tilted slightly back, often make fine wrist shooters. Once in place, their wrist simply relaxes (at the right time), letting their forearm FALL back into position. A complex two-step act blends into a natural, smooth, one-step motion, needing little thought. A little flick pulls your forearm forward for the delivery.

Using a catapult shot the wrist trails both ways as your forearm goes first. With the wrist shot the forearm trails as your wrist leads.

At first, a wrist shot may appear complex because you must use new muscle groups to pivot your wrist. A catapult throw forces your wrist to swivel and follow the arm (like a whip) with no effort, right at the target. With the wrist shot, you must guide a dart more. Errors also produce wobbly, erratic throws.

Perfecting this method, you gain greater awareness, feeling more in control. Sensing control helps you relax and play more easily.

Gaining poise using a wrist shot, try precocking your fingers. A hard motion to control, it adds zip to your dart and a minimum arc.

Presetting fingers and wrist may further improve this method. Bringing your arm back, at the release point, 'pull the trigger.' Try both ways.

'X' THE SPOT: An unusual, but sensible way to place a dart before throwing is to 'X' the spot. Start with some hand or dart part always touching a spot on your head or body. The pluses! A longer stroke, like a rifle, is more accurate than a pistol. Players using more caution (to avoid injury), slow their throws. Throwing at an even speed is easier. Staying still at the line, your dart always starts from the same point. Contact turns your mind from the details, allowing the brain to work freely.

I saw two pros using this system. One lightly brushes his cheek with the dart's flight. Another pro touches the flight to her forehead. In our league, a player brushes his knuckles across the chin. Possible spots are many.

Precise darters who stand still can best use this touch system. Yet, it would slow players who throw too fast or hard. I admit few darters do (or even can) wisely, use spotting. Repeated tries gave me nothing, but this system might provide you with a big lift.

149 **YOU ARE THE ONE:** Success depends on you, no one else! No matter what book, player or other help used, _YOU_ are in charge. Simply reading or taking advice will never make you a dartist! Even this book is useless unless you apply its ideas during each practice session and match.

Untested ideas are of no value. Never forget! You and your dart routine are unique. No one else does, or could play the same. The world's best dartist's methods will be of little use to you. Finding what works best (FOR YOU) may take time and work. Giving up easily and not trying, growth is slow, if at all.

You may be content at your present skill level and not care about getting better, which is fine. You are unlikely to be a big asset to your team or mates, though. When the team and longtime friends move up you may not go along. Again, if you are enjoying your Darts, this is okay.

YOUTH DARTS: A recent and long overdue trend **150** is Darts for youths. Started about ten years ago, teen and preteen leagues are now worldwide in scope. Bringing young people into Darts is vital! Sadly, non-drinkers may not

Tom Daly

know the game exists. Non drinkers, like I, may spend a lifetime totally unaware. I regret daily missing the sport in my teens. Early discovery would have changed my life. Finding Darts and playing well at an age when most stop (50), I wonder how good I could have been.

Starting and keeping a healthy youth program is difficult even with financing and sponsors. It needs a crew of loyal adults willing to stay for the long term. You may ask, "Are there enough youngsters to bother?" Most children show an interest in sports, but few are jocks. Even large schools with very active athletic programs do well to draw enough players to justify them.

We maintain sports programs because of the proven leadership quality athletes' gain. Why deprive those students lacking in physical strength, the same benefits? In my experience, Darts offers the same pluses, in some growth areas, more.

To cover youth Darts completely would require too many pages! Any interested persons or groups please write. I will forward all letters to the area's ruling body.

YOUTH DART DIRECTORS PLEASE TAKE NOTE! Send us detailed info so, if possible, we might share any book profits with your groups.

151 ZIP YOUR LIPS: Learn to keep your mouth closed, while playing Darts. Some darters think while their side shoots that they can say what they want. NOT SO! Cheering a favored team or urging mates on is perfectly okay and in the spirit of Darts. Slyly cutting down the other team or its players is a low act! Direct acid remarks are absolute no-nos. Rude players have very short dart careers.

If you lose, because of actions by a rival's team or its fans, shake hands and smile broadly as you say "GOOD DARTS!" Smart dartists get the point. Steaming inside, say nothing. Never let others see anger. Showing this bothers you only invites more.

The best answer. Above all, never become hostile! Simply inform their captain more barbs mean a protest of every match involved. Today, most leagues ban verbal abuse. Do file a

Mike Manos

protest! The league will now watch this team's actions closely. Not filing says, "you got away with it." Not fearing losing points, insults continue to grow.

If captains cannot quiet culprits or others who are not team members, ask management to eject them. ◄151
Failing this, ask to reschedule or protest the entire match. Let the league deal with discipline.

Tainted wins never satisfy. You gain no pride in winning matches decided by a big mouth, just embarrassment. Winning, by using skill, is the only way. Do not allow anyone (even mates) to dig others with words like these: "She can get in, but not out" or "He's waiting for you." Both about as subtle as a razor-sharp ax and cut as deep! Oddly, hecklers are the first to scream upon hearing similar words when they are at the line. Hazing always returns tenfold.

Light, good-natured banter during a match is a big plus. Exchange of this sort gives joy to all. Problems arise when anyone tries to use words to control a match's result. Teach anyone not knowing any better. Another point, avoid horseplay taking care no one gets hurt. Too many fool around in practice by giving pal(s) a friendly push as they throw. A stray dart could hurt others. Keep your hands to yourself!

A team's captain is liable for his player's acts. Yet, the entire team suffers for any wrongs. Number the days if you stay the villain.

152 **DARTS TODAY:** My own views, after thirteen years of playing in two leagues. One the worlds largest. Darts is healthy, but needs some basic changes to grow stronger, faster.

Where is the sport lacking? To start, we need more programs

Barry S. Levine

Louis P Sparanges, DMD

Alan Goldberg, Ed. D.

Ling-Nah Su Ph.D.

109

and outlets for youths. The game must expand from (not leave) pubs and bars, providing areas for all who cannot or do not wish to enter them.

We must tackle the shortage and neglect of women. Many men do not take women seriously and scare them off. Darts is now too much of an old boy's club. Leagues should require at least two or three women on every team and allow them to compete with each other if they wish. Welcome women! Darts will boom.

Other needed steps: Erase profanity, rude behavior and hazing of players. Twice and your out—period! Stop the practice of superior players on low division teams. Move up darters winning so many individual matches or percentage of total games. Also, devise fairer pairing of darters by skill levels, especially during play-off bouts. A new US-wide league successfully uses a handicap system. Allow all-star points on third leg, the hardest time to hit them.

Finally! We stress winning too much. We should ◀152 reward those players, who improve most, try the hardest, are the best sports, etc. Winning is great, but should not be the only end. ***Make having fun number one!*** Many will think these minor bothers at best. Yet, fixing our current problems will greatly improve Darts.

DARTS FUTURE: Again, this is my own slant. Darts is now at a decisive turning point. Political forces may destroy the game at the national and world levels if sanity fails to rule. Denying any darter, at any skill level, the choice of where, when and with whom they can play will never benefit anyone.

Darts cannot hope for Olympic Games entry until a unified body. Locally, Darts will flourish despite the wars waged at higher ranks.

LAST—BUT MOST IMPORTANT

The names framed in this book were vital to its creation. Each taught me values for darters. They were mates, sponsors or sources. ALL true friends! Sadly, some are gone.

| *Brian O'Connell* | *Sean O'Connell* |

One I have not met. Call me to add or fix. 508-366-0014 at publication. Everyone listed has a free copy coming. Call if you have not received yours.   THANK YOU ALL!

The Forgotten Few

FLIGHT PROFILES (See article #60)

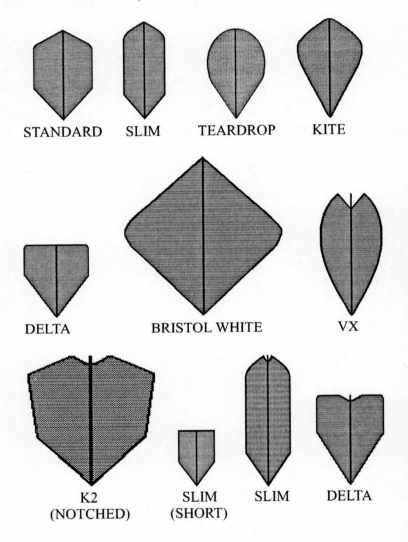

STANDARD   SLIM   TEARDROP   KITE

DELTA   BRISTOL WHITE   VX

K2
(NOTCHED)   SLIM
(SHORT)   SLIM   DELTA

BOOK PURCHASE BONUS NO. 1
THE PRO DART (PRACTICE) PLATFORM™ PLANS—A $5 VALUE

MATERIAL: (From Hardware store)
- One piece of 12 by 24 inch A/C grade or better ¾" plywood.
- Nine Brainerd #434XC (or equal) rubber bumpers, with screws.
- One sheet of 100 grit Aluminum Oxide Sandpaper.

NEEDED TOOLS:
> Pencil - Black Felt Marker - Ruler/straightedge - A steel-tipped Dart

CONSTRUCTION: See Sketches on following pages
1. Sand all plywood edges and corners smooth.
2. **See Sketch A**—On plywood's best side (TOP): Using a straightedge, mark one end as shown with felt marker.
3. **See Sketch B**—On plywood's rougher side (BOTTOM): Draw three (3) <u>pencil lines</u>, marking the center of each.

Using Sketch C
> 3A. Locate and mark six (6) more points on all three (3) lines.
>
> A total of seven (7) on each of these <u>pencil lines</u>.
>
> 3B. Push a dart's tip about ¼" straight into the twenty one (21) premarked spots—for pilot holes.
>
> 3C. Mount three (3) bumpers on each line with screws.
>
> Take care not to overtighten screws. To fix a stripped hole, jam in a wooden toothpick and break it off flush at surface.

Do not paint or in any way alter the plywood's natural surface traction!

PLATFORM IS COMPLETE. To use, see article #112

SKETCH-A (TOP)

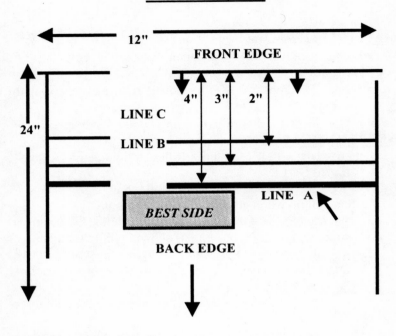

NOTES:

This sketch is not to scale.

For safety, line 'A' should be wider and or drawn with a **RED** marker. A constant warning that going over it, the platform will tip without weight on your back leg.

SKETCH-B (BOTTOM)

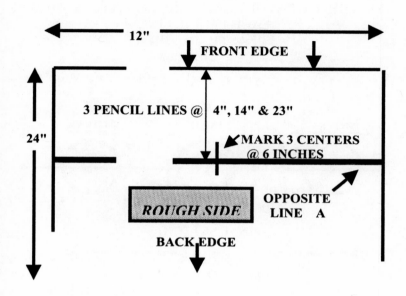

NOTES:
   This sketch is not to scale.
   Two omitted lines are identical to the 4".

SKETCH-C
PILOT HOLE LAYOUT AND BUMPER STEPS (SAME AT
EACH PENCIL LINE)
3 PLASTIC BUMPERS

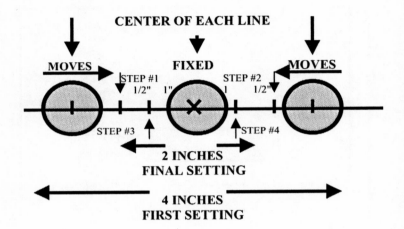

CENTER OF EACH LINE

MOVES   FIXED   MOVES

STEP #1   STEP #2

1/2"   1"   1   1/2"

STEP #3   STEP #4

**2 INCHES
FINAL SETTING**

**4 INCHES
FIRST SETTING**

NOTES:

This sketch is not to scale.

PLATFORM CAUTIONS!

Do not use if dizzy, disoriented or unstable for any reason at all.

Keep out of children's reach. Do not use while barefooted.

Do not use for any other purpose. If plywood warps—replace it.

The builder is responsible for all defects. Inspect the platform often.

Made and used as above, the PRO DART (PRACTICE) PLATFORM™ will work as claimed. All other obligations or liabilities excluded, including liability for consequential damages.

BOOK PURCHASE BONUS NO. 2
SHAFTITE™ FORMULA—A $1.50 VALUE
Set it & forget it, works for years.

The invisible gripper that securely holds any 2BA dart shaft.

I created this useful product to fill a need lacking at the time. Now, I give it to all for the years of joy Darts gave me. Durable, cheap, easy to use and, most important, it works.

Most hardware stores carry rubber 'O' ring stock in various widths. Buy a 6-inch piece of the <u>straight</u> BLACK 1/8-inch size. The RED stock is too soft! This should last most players forever. Be sure the diameter is exact or at worst a tad less.

HOW TO USE SHAFTITE™
- ◆ REMOVE SHAFT FROM DART.
- ◆ PUSH SHAFTITE™ TO BOTTOM OF TAPPED HOLE.
- ◆ USING A RAZOR, CUT OFF FLUSH.
- ◆ REMOVE PIECE FROM HOLE AND TRIM AS SHOWN BELOW.
- ◆ PLACE FINAL PIECE IN DART AND SEAT SHAFT TIGHTLY.

TIPS: A quarter is 1/16-inch thick. Use 1/4-inch 'O' ring stock for brass darts.

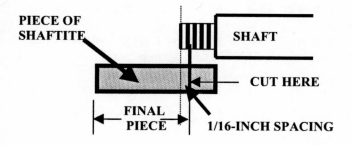

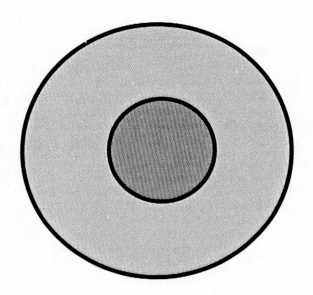

CRICKET BASICS

CRICKET is a game of action and reaction.

To win you must close all numbers first and be even or ahead on points.

Three marks on a number (first), _**open**_ it to scoring by opener.

Three marks on a number (second), _**close**_ it to all scoring.

Above all else **STAY CALM** when behind!

CRICKET STRATEGIES

Strive for a minimum of three marks per turn and expect the same from opponent(s).

Use total marks scored to compare game position.

Play offensively. Chasing (closing behind an opener) is defensive and a losing move.

Take control; open numbers 1st, close later. Always score FIRST!

When in doubt, POINT! Scoring gives the greatest bang per dart, BUT, not in excess!

IF possible, close bulls early for a comeback, to create a barrier or psych-out opponent(s).

Close open numbers (including bulls) only with a good lead and extra darts.

You win or lose CRICKET with single marks. Aim for triples but expect singles.

Some of these pointers are more important, but use them all.

__Once playing a few CRICKET games, even non-players will quickly grasp these points.__

This book belongs to

_____*A WINNER!

Become a winner too! The perfect gift for all those winning darters you know. Order an electronic book or hard copy online at this web site.
http://www.1stbooks.com.

ABOUT THE AUTHOR

The author, at 50, began playing Darts in 1985 and was frustrated by the total lack of available advice. He then spent 14 years analyzing all its physical and mental aspects. He now offers his knowledge to all present and future players of this fascinating sport.

Printed in the United States
39097LVS00001B/148